URBAN TRAILS
BELLINGHAM

URBAN TRAILS

TRAILS

BELLINGHAM

Chuckanut Mountains
Western Whatcom · Skagit Valley

CRAIG ROMANO

MOUNTAINEERS
BOOKS

Mountaineers Books is the publishing division of
The Mountaineers, an organization founded in 1906
and dedicated to the exploration, preservation, and
enjoyment of outdoor and wilderness areas.

1001 SW Klickitat Way, Suite 201, Seattle, WA 98134
800.553.4453, www.mountaineersbooks.org

Printed in China
Distributed in the United Kingdom by Cordee, www.cordee.co.uk
First edition, 2017

Copy Editor: Kristi Hein, Pictures & Words Editorial Services
Design: Jen Grable
Layout: Jennifer Shontz, www.redshoedesign.com
Cartographer: Lohnes+Wright
All photographs by author unless otherwise noted.
Cover Photo: *Lake Padden Park*
Frontispiece: *Totem pole along Whatcom Creek Trail*

Library of Congress Cataloging-in-Publication Data on file

Mountaineers Books titles may be purchased for corporate, educational, or
other promotional sales, and our authors are available for a wide range of
events. For information on special discounts or booking an author, contact
our customer service at 800-553-4453 or mbooks@mountaineersbooks.org.

ISBN (paperback): 978-1-68051-024-9
ISBN (ebook): 978-1-68051-025-6

CONTENTS

ANACORTES AND FIDALGO ISLAND

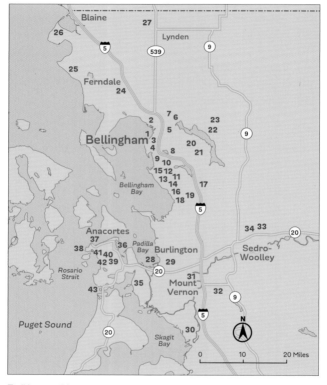

Blaine
26
27
Lynden
5
539
9
25
Ferndale
24
7 6
23
2
5
22
Bellingham
1 3
20
4
21
8
9
10
15 12
13 14
11
Bellingham
16
17
Bay
18
19
5
34 33
Anacortes
37
20
36 Padilla
Bay
Burlington
38
41 40
28 29
42 39
Sedro-
Woolley
Rosario
20
Strait
35
31
43
Mount
32
Vernon
9
Puget Sound
5
N
20
30
Skagit
Bay
0   10   20 Miles

Trail Locator Map

TRAILS AT A GLANCE

Trail and/or Park	Distance	Walk	Hike	Run	Kids	Dogs
BELLINGHAM						
1. South Bay Trail	5 miles roundtrip	•		•	•	•
2. Bay to Baker Trail Parks	more than 6 miles of trails	•		•	•	•
3. Sehome Hill Arboretum	more than 6 miles of trails	•	•	•	•	•
4. Connelly Creek Trail	2 miles roundtrip	•		•	•	•
5. Whatcom Falls	5.5 miles of trails	•	•	•	•	•
6. Railroad Trail	3.2 miles one-way	•		•	•	•
7. Klipsun Trail and Northridge Park	3.2 miles of trails	•		•	•	•
8. Lake Padden Park	more than 9 miles of trails	•	•	•	•	•
CHUCKANUT MOUNTAINS						
9. Interurban Trail	6.6 miles one-way	•	•	•	•	•
10. Arroyo Park and Chuckanut Falls	2 miles roundtrip		•	•	•	•
11. Pine and Cedar Lakes	5.2 miles roundtrip		•	•		•
12. Raptor Ridge	8.3 miles roundtrip		•	•		•
13. Fragrance Lake	4.4 miles roundtrip		•	•	•	•
14. Lost Lake	up to 9.8 miles roundtrip		•	•		•
15. Chuckanut Ridge	10.8 miles roundtrip		•	•		•
16. Clayton Beach	1.2 miles roundtrip		•			•
17. Squires Lake	2 miles of trails	•	•	•	•	•

Trail and/or Park	Distance	Walk	Hike	Run	Kids	Dogs
18. Oyster Dome	6.2 miles roundtrip		•	•		•
19. Lizard and Lily Lakes	7.5 miles roundtrip		•	•	•	•
WESTERN WHATCOM COUNTY						
20. Stimpson Family Nature Reserve	4 miles of trails		•		•	
21. Lookout Mountain Forest Preserve	more than 4 miles of trails		•	•	•	•
22. Lake Whatcom Park: Hertz Trail	6.2 miles roundtrip	•	•	•	•	•
23. Lake Whatcom Park: Stewart Mountain	9 miles roundtrip		•	•		•
24. Hovander Homestead and Tennant Lake Parks	4 miles of trails	•	•	•	•	•
25. Point Whitehorn Marine Reserve	0.7 mile trail 2 mile beach		•		•	
26. Semiahmoo Spit	0.8 mile trail 1 mile beach	•		•	•	•
27. Berthusen Park	7 miles of trails	•	•	•	•	•
SKAGIT VALLEY						
28. Padilla Bay Dike Trail	4.8 miles roundtrip	•	•	•	•	•
29. Skagit Airport Trails	up to 10.1 miles of trails	•		•	•	•
30. Skagit Wildlife Area: Headquarters Unit	1.9 miles of trails	•	•		•	•
31. Mount Vernon Riverwalk	2 miles roundtrip	•		•	•	•
32. Little Mountain Park	more than 10 miles of trail	•	•	•	•	•
33. Northern State Recreation Area	more than 5 miles of trail	•	•	•	•	•
34. Cascade Trail	up to 22.5 miles one-way	•	•	•	•	•

Trail and/or Park	Distance	Walk	Hike	Run	Kids	Dogs
ANACORTES AND FIDALGO ISLAND						
35. Kukutali Preserve (Kiket Island)	2 miles of trail	•	•		•	
36. Tommy Thompson Trail	3.3 miles one-way	•		•	•	•
37. Guemes Channel and Ship Harbor Trails	2.7 miles of trail	•		•	•	•
38. Washington Park	more than 4 miles of trails	•	•	•	•	•
39a. Sugar Loaf	2.5 miles of trail		•	•	•	•
39b. Mount Erie	5.2 miles of trails	•	•	•		•
39c. Whistle Lake	4.3 miles roundtrip	•	•	•	•	•
40. Heart Lake	3 miles roundtrip	•	•	•	•	•
41. Little Cranberry Lake	1.9 miles roundtrip	•	•	•	•	•
42. Big Beaver Pond and Mitten Pond	2.7 miles roundtrip	•	•	•	•	•
43. Deception Pass State Park	more than 40 miles of trails	•	•	•	•	•

INTRODUCTION
TRAILS FOR FUN AND FITNESS
IN YOUR BIG BACKYARD

LET'S FACE IT: WHETHER YOU'RE a hiker, walker, or runner, life can get in the way when it comes to putting in time on the trail. Far too often, it's hard for most of us to set aside an hour—never mind a day, or even longer—to hit the trails of our favorite parks and forests across the state. But that doesn't mean we can't get out on the trail more frequently. Right in and near our own communities are thousands of acres of parks and nature preserves containing hundreds of miles of trails. And we can visit these pocket wildernesses, urban and urban-fringe parks and preserves, greenbelts, and trail corridors on a whim—for an hour or two—without having to drive far. Some of these places we can visit without even driving at all—hopping on the bus instead, which lessens our carbon footprint while giving us more time to relax away from our hurried schedules.

Urban Trails: Bellingham focuses on the myriad of trails, parks, and preserves within the urban, suburban, and rural fringe areas around Bellingham, Anacortes, and Mount Vernon in the Skagit Valley. You'll find trails to beaches, old-growth forests, lakeshores, riverfronts, shorelines, wildlife-rich

Author and assistant on a winter hike at Squires Lake

wetlands, rolling hills, scenic vistas, meadows, historic sites, and vibrant communities. While often we equate hiking trails with the state's wildernesses and forests, there are plenty of areas of natural beauty and accessible trails in the midst of our population centers. The routes included here are designed to show you where you can go for a nice run, long walk, or quick hike right in your own backyard.

This guide has two missions. One is to promote fitness and get you outside more often! A trip to Mount Rainier, North Cascades, or Olympic national parks can be a major undertaking for many of us. But a quick outdoor getaway to a local park or trail can be done almost anytime—before work, during a lunch break, after work, or when we don't feel like fighting traffic and driving for miles. And nearly all of these trails are available year-round, so you can walk, run, or hike every day by utilizing the trails within your own neighborhood. If you feel you are not getting outside enough or getting enough exercise, this book can help you achieve a healthier lifestyle.

Mission number two of this guide is to promote the local parks, preserves, and trails within and near our urban areas. More than 4.5 million people (65 percent of the state's population) call the greater Puget Sound area home. While conservationists continue to promote protection of our state's large roadless wild corners—and that is still important—it's equally important that we promote the preservation of natural areas and develop more trails and greenbelts right where people live. Why? For one thing, the Puget Sound area contains unique and threatened ecosystems that deserve to be protected as much as our wilder remote places. And we need to have usable and accessible trails where people live, work, and spend the majority of their time. Urban trails and parks allow folks to be outside and bond with nature on a regular basis. They help us cut our carbon footprint by giving us access to recreation without burning excessive gallons of fuel to reach a destination. They make it easier for us to commit to regular

The old trestle over Whatcom Creek at Whatcom Creek Falls Park

exercise programs, giving us safe and agreeable places to walk, run, and hike. And urban trails and parks also offer disadvantaged populations—folks who may not have cars and/or the means to travel to one of our national parks or forests—a chance to experience nature and a healthy life-style too. As the greater Puget Sound area continues to grow in population and become increasingly more developed, it is all the more important that we support the expansion of our urban parks and trails.

So get out there, get fit, and have fun! And don't forget to advocate for more trails and parks.

HOW TO USE THIS GUIDE

THIS EASY-TO-USE GUIDE PROVIDES YOU with enough details to get out on the trail with confidence while leaving enough room for your own personal discovery. I have walked, hiked, and/or run every mile of trails described here, and the directions and advice are accurate and up-to-date. Conditions can and do change, however, so make sure you check on the status of a park or trail before you go.

THE DESTINATIONS

This book includes forty-three destinations, covering trails in and around Bellingham, the Chuckanut Mountains, Mount Vernon, and Anacortes. Each one begins with the park and/or trail name. Next is a block of information detailing the following:

Distance. Here you will find roundtrip mileage (unless otherwise noted) if the route describes a single trail, or the total mileage of trails within the park, preserve, or greenway

A rare snowfall makes for good cross-country skiing at the Northern State Recreation Area.

if the route gives an overview of the destination's trail system. Note that while I have measured most of the trails in this book with GPS and have consulted maps and governing land agencies, the distance stated may not always be exact—but it'll be pretty darn close.

Elevation gain. For individual trails, elevation gain is for the *cumulative* difference on the route (and return), meaning not only the difference between the high and low points on the trail, but also for all other significant changes in elevation along the way. For destinations that feature multiple routes, such as in a trail network within a park, the elevation gain applies to the steepest trail on the route.

High point. The high point is the highest elevation of the trail or trail system described. Almost all of the trails in the book are at a relatively low elevation, ensuring mostly snow-free winter access.

Difficulty. This factor is based not only on length and elevation gain of a trail or trails, but also on the type of tread and surface area of the trail(s). Most of the trails in this book are easy or moderate for the average hiker, walker, or runner. Depending on your level of fitness, you may find the trails more or less difficult than described.

Fitness. This description denotes whether the trail is best for hikers, walkers, or runners. Generally, paved trails will be of more interest to walkers and runners, while rough, hilly trails will appeal more to hikers. Of course you are free to hike, walk, or run (unless running is specifically prohibited) on any of the trails in this book.

Family-friendly. Here you'll find notes on a trail's or park's suitability for children and any cautions to be aware of, such as cliffs, heavy mountain bike use, and so on. Some trails may be noted as ADA-accessible and suitable for jogging strollers.

Dog-friendly. This denotes whether dogs are allowed on the trail and what regulations (such as leashed and under control) apply.

Off-leash areas offer dogs a chance to romp.

Amenities. The featured park's amenities can include privies, drinking water, benches, interpretive signs or displays, shelters, learning centers, campgrounds, and dog poop–bag dispensers, to name a few.

Management. The name(s) of the bodies or agencies responsible for managing the area.

Contact/map. Here you'll find contact info for getting current trail conditions. All websites and phone numbers for trail and park managers or governing agencies can be found in Appendix I. These websites will often direct you to trail and park maps; in some cases, a better or supplemental map is noted (such as Green Trails).

GPS. GPS coordinates are provided for the main trailhead to help get you to the trail.

Before you go. This section notes any fees or permits required, hours the park or preserve is open (if limited), closures, and any other special concerns.

Next, I describe how to get to the trailhead via your own vehicle or by public transport if available.

GETTING THERE. Driving: Provides directions to the trail-head—generally from the nearest large town or major road and often from more than one direction—and also parking information. **Transit:** If the trailhead is served by public trans-portation, this identifies the bus agency and line.

EACH HIKE begins with an overview of the featured park and/or trail, highlighting its setting and character, with notes on the property's conservation history.

GET MOVING. This section describes the route or trails and what you might find on your hike, walk, or run; it may note additional highlights beyond the trail itself such as points of historical interest.

GO FARTHER. Here you'll find suggestions for making your hike, walk, or run longer within the featured park—or perhaps by combining this trip with an adjacent or nearby park or trail.

PERMITS, REGULATIONS, AND PARK FEES

Most of the trails and parks described in this book are man-aged by county and city parks departments, requiring no per-mits or fees. Destinations managed by Washington State Parks and the Washington State Department of Natural Resources (DNR) require a day-use fee in the form of the Discover Pass (www.discoverpass.wa.gov) for vehicle access. A Discover Pass costs $10 per vehicle per day or $30 for up to two vehicles annually. (Note: If you make more than three visits in a year, the annual pass is the way to go). You can purchase the pass online, at many retail outlets, or better yet, from a state park office to avoid the $5 handling fee. Each hike in this book clearly states if a fee is charged or a pass is required.

Regulations such as whether dogs are allowed or a park has restricted hours or is closed for certain occasions (such as during high fire danger or for wildlife management) are clearly spelled out in each trail's information block.

Mount Baker provides a backdrop for pintails in Drayton Harbor

ROAD AND TRAIL CONDITIONS

In general, trails change little year to year. But change can and does occur, and sometimes very quickly. A heavy storm can wash out sections of trail or access road in moments. Wind storms can blow down multiple trees across trails, making paths impassable. Lack of adequate funding is also responsible for trail neglect and degradation. For some of the wilder destinations in this book, it is wise to contact the appropriate land manager after a significant weather event to check on current trail and road conditions.

On the topic of trail conditions, it is vital that we acknowledge the countless volunteers who donate tens of thousands of hours to trail maintenance each year. The Washington Trails Association (WTA) alone coordinates upward of 100,000 hours of volunteer trail maintenance each year. But there is always a need for more. Our trail system faces ever-increasing threats, including lack of adequate trail funding. Consider joining one or more of the trail and conservation groups listed in Appendix II.

OUTDOORS ETHICS

Strong, positive outdoors ethics include making sure you leave the trail (and park) in as good a condition as you found it—or even better. Get involved with groups and organizations that safeguard, watchdog, and advocate for land protection. And get on the phone and keyboard, and let land managers and public officials know how important protecting lands and trails is to you.

All of us who recreate in Washington's natural areas have a moral obligation and responsibility to respect and protect our natural heritage. Everything we do on the planet has an impact—and we should strive to have as little negative impact as possible. The Leave No Trace Center for Outdoors Ethics is an educational, nonpartisan, nonprofit organization that was developed for responsible enjoyment and active

Trail at Squalicum Harbor Marina in Bellingham

stewardship of the outdoors. Its program helps educate outdoor enthusiasts about their recreational impacts and recommends techniques to prevent and minimize such impacts. While geared toward backcountry use, many Leave No Trace (LNT) principles are also sound advice for urban and urban fringe parks too, including: plan ahead, dispose of waste properly, and be considerate of other visitors. Visit www.lnt.org to learn more.

TRAIL ETIQUETTE
We need to be sensitive not only to the environment surrounding our trails, but to other trail users as well. Some of the trails in this book are also open to mountain bikers and equestrians.

Sunset over Semihamoo Bay from Blaine Marine Park

When you encounter other trail users, whether they are hikers, runners, bicyclists, or horseback riders, the only hard-and-fast rule is to follow common sense and exercise simple courtesy. With this Golden Rule of Trail Etiquette firmly in mind, here are other things you can do during trail encounters to make everyone's trip more enjoyable:

- **Right-of-way.** When meeting bicyclists or horseback riders, those of us on foot should move off the trail. This is because hikers, walkers, and runners are more mobile and flexible than other users, making it easier for us to quickly step off the trail.

- **Encountering horses.** When meeting horseback riders specifically, step off the downhill side of the trail unless the terrain makes this difficult or dangerous. In that case, move to the uphill side of the trail, but crouch down a bit so you do not tower over the horses' heads. Also, make yourself visible so as not to spook the big beastie, and talk in a normal voice to the riders. This calms the horses. If walking with a dog, keep your buddy under control.

- **Stay on trails.** Don't cut switchbacks, take shortcuts, or make new trails; all lead to erosion and unsightly trail degradation.

- **Obey the rules specific to the trail or park you are visiting.** Many trails are closed to certain types of use, including dogs and mountain bikes.

- **Hiking, walking, or running with dogs.** Trail users who bring dogs should have their dog on a leash or under very strict voice command at all times. And if leashes are required, then this DOES apply to you. Many trail users who have had negative encounters with dogs (actually with the dog owners) on the trail are not fond of, or are even afraid of, encountering dogs. Respect their right *not* to be approached by your darling pooch. A well-behaved leashed dog, however, can certainly help warm up these folks to a canine encounter.

Bald eagles are commonly seen throughout the Skagit and Nooksack valleys.

- **Avoid disturbing wildlife.** Observe from a distance, resisting the urge to move closer to wildlife (use your telephoto lens). This not only keeps you safer but also prevents the animal from having to exert itself unnecessarily to flee from you.
- **Take only photographs.** Leave all natural features and historic artifacts as you found them for others to enjoy.
- **Never roll rocks off of trails or cliffs.** Gravity increases the impact of falling rocks exponentially, and you risk endangering lives below you.
- **Mind the music.** Not everyone (usually almost no one) wants to hear your blaring music. If you like listening to music while you run, hike, or walk, wear headphones and respect other trail users' right to peace and quiet—and to listen to nature's music.

HUNTING

Some of the destinations in this book (such as Blanchard Mountain) are open to hunting. Season dates vary, but generally in Washington big-game hunting begins in early August and ends in late November. Also, bird hunting is popular in the Skagit Valley during the winter months. While using trails in areas frequented by hunters, it is best to make yourself visible by donning an orange cap and vest. If hiking with a dog, your buddy should wear an orange vest too.

BEARS AND COUGARS

Washington harbors healthy populations of black bears, found in many of the parks and preserves along the urban fringe. If you encounter a bear while hiking, you'll usually just catch a glimpse of its bear behind. But occasionally the bruin may actually want to get a look at *you*.

To avoid an un-*bear*-able encounter, practice bear-aware prudence: Always keep a safe distance. Remain calm, do not look a bear in the eyes, speak in a low tone, and do not run from it. Hold your arms out to appear as big as possible. Slowly move away. The bear may bluff-charge—do not run. If it does charge, lie down and play dead, protecting your head and neck. Usually the bear will leave once he perceives he is not threatened. If he does attack, fight back using fists, rocks, trekking poles, or bear spray if you are carrying it.

Our state also supports a healthy population of *Felix concolor*. While cougar encounters are extremely rare, they do occur—even occasionally in parks and preserves on the urban fringe. Cougars are cats—they're curious. They may follow hikers but rarely (almost never) attack adult humans. Minimize contact by not hiking or running alone and by avoiding carrion. If you do encounter a cougar, remember the big cat is looking for prey that can't or won't fight back. Do not run, as this may trigger its prey instinct. Stand up and face it. If you appear aggressive, the cougar will probably back down. Wave your arms, trekking poles, or a jacket over your head to appear bigger, and maintain eye contact. Pick up children and small dogs and back away slowly if you can do so safely, not taking your eyes off of it. If it attacks, throw things at it. Shout loudly. If it gets close, whack it with your trekking pole, fighting back aggressively.

WATER AND GEAR
While most of the trails in this book can be enjoyed without much preparation or gear, it is always a good idea to bring water, even if you're just out for a quick walk or run. Even better, carry a small pack with water, a few snacks, sunglasses, and a rain jacket.

THE TEN ESSENTIALS
If you are heading out for a longer adventure—perhaps an all-day hike in the Chuckanut Mountains—consider packing **The Ten Essentials**, items that are good to have on hand in an emergency:

- Navigation. Carry a map of the area you plan to be in and know how to read it. A cellphone and/or GPS unit are good to have along too.
- Sun protection. Even on wet days, carry sunscreen and sunglasses; you never know when the clouds will lift, and you can easily sunburn near bodies of water.
- Insulation. Storms can and do blow in rapidly. Carry raingear, wind gear, and extra layers.
- Illumination. If caught out after dark, you'll be glad you have a headlamp or flashlight so you can follow the trail home.
- First-aid supplies. At the very least, your kit should include: bandages, gauze, scissors, tape, tweezers, pain relievers, antiseptics, and perhaps a small manual.
- Fire. While being forced to spend the night out is not likely on these trails, a campfire could provide welcome

Running on the Nooksack River Trail

warmth in an emergency; keep matches dry in a zip-lock bag.

- **Repair kit and tools.** A pocketknife or multitool can come in handy, as can basic repair items such as nylon cord, safety pins, a small roll of duct tape, and a small tube of superglue.
- **Nutrition.** Pack a handful of nuts or sports bars for emergency pick-me-ups.
- **Hydration.** Bring enough water to keep you hydrated, and for longer treks consider a means of water purification.
- **Emergency shelter.** This can be as simple as a garbage bag or a rain poncho to double as an emergency tarp.

TRAILHEAD CONCERNS

By and large, our parks and trails are safe places. Common sense and vigilance, however, are still in order. This is true for all trail users, but particularly so for solo ones. Be aware of your surroundings at all times. Let someone know when and where you're headed out.

Car break-ins are a common occurrence at some of our parks and trailheads. Never leave anything of value in your vehicle while out on the trail. Take your wallet and smartphone with you. A duffel bag on the back seat may contain dirty T-shirts, but a thief may think there's a laptop in it. Save yourself the hassle of returning to a busted window by not giving criminals a reason to clout your car.

If you arrive at a trailhead and someone looks suspicious, don't discount your intuition. If something doesn't feel right, it probably isn't. Take action by leaving the place or situation

A NOTE ABOUT SAFETY

Safety is an important concern in all outdoor activities. No guidebook can alert you to every hazard or anticipate the limitations of every reader. Therefore, the descriptions of roads, trails, routes, and natural features in this book are not representations that a particular place or excursion will be safe for your party. When you follow any of the routes described in this book, you assume responsibility for your own safety. Under normal conditions, such excursions require the usual attention to traffic, road and trail conditions, weather, terrain, the capabilities of your party, and other factors. Because many of the lands in this book are subject to development and/or change of ownership, conditions may have changed since this book was written that make your use of some of these routes unwise. Always check for current conditions, obey posted private property signs, and avoid confrontations with property owners or managers. Keeping informed on current conditions and exercising common sense are the keys to a safe, enjoyable outing.

—Mountaineers Books

promptly. If the person behaves inappropriately or aggressively, take notes on their appearance and their vehicle's make and license plate, and report their behavior to the authorities. Do not confront the person; leave and go to another trail.

No need to be paranoid, though, for our trails and parks are far safer than most urban areas. Just use a little common sense and vigilance while you're out and about.

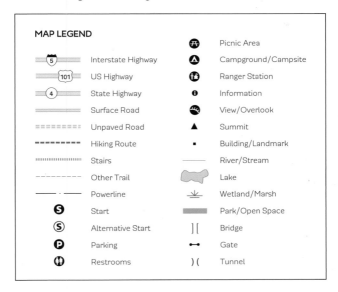

MAP LEGEND

5	Interstate Highway	(picnic)	Picnic Area
101	US Highway	(campground)	Campground/Campsite
4	State Highway	(ranger)	Ranger Station
	Surface Road	Information	Information
	Unpaved Road	(view)	View/Overlook
	Hiking Route	▲	Summit
	Stairs	▪	Building/Landmark
	Other Trail		River/Stream
	Powerline		Lake
S	Start		Wetland/Marsh
S	Alternative Start		Park/Open Space
P	Parking	] [	Bridge
R	Restrooms	•—	Gate
		) (	Tunnel

Next page: *Evening light at Lake Padden*

BELLINGHAM

You'd be hard-pressed to find a more dramatic location within the state than Bellingham's: situated in Northwestern Washington, along the shore of the island-spangled Salish Sea and within the shadow of Washington's snowiest volcano, Mount Baker. Whatcom County seat and home of Western Washington University, this city of 85,000 sits between the Seattle and Vancouver, BC, metropolitan areas, yet it's surrounded by forest, farm, and water.

Long cherished by its residents for its healthy, active, and out-doorsy lifestyle, Bellingham is "Washington's Boulder," but without the Colorado city's ample sunshine! Yet even though it is one of the cloudiest cities in America, the weather here is generally agreeable. And young people and retirees from throughout the Pacific North-west and the entire country continue to make Bellingham their home. It is lauded by many publications and organizations for being one of America's best places to live, safest cities, greenest cities, dog-friendliest cities, most adventurous cities, best paddling cities, best places to retire—and, might I add, one of America's top trail towns. Bellingham contains and is surrounded by thousands of acres of parkland interconnected by one of the largest trail networks in the Northwest. Hiking, running, and walking is a way of life here.

1 South Bay Trail

DISTANCE:	5 miles roundtrip
ELEVATION GAIN:	75 feet
HIGH POINT:	75 feet
DIFFICULTY:	Easy
FITNESS:	Walkers, runners
FAMILY-FRIENDLY:	Yes, and stroller-friendly
DOG-FRIENDLY:	On leash
AMENITIES:	Restrooms, water, concession, benches
CONTACT/MAPS:	City of Bellingham Parks
GPS:	N 48° 43.883" W 122° 30.088"

GETTING THERE

Driving: From downtown Bellingham, follow State Street west for 0.6 mile to a traffic circle. Proceed on Boulevard Street for 0.8 mile and merge back onto State Street. Continue for 0.4 mile, turning right onto Bayview Drive. Proceed 0.3 mile to Boulevard Park and trailhead parking.

From Mount Vernon, follow I-5 north to Fairhaven exit 250. Then head 1.3 miles west on Old Fairhaven Parkway (State Route 11) and turn right onto 12th Street. Continue north on 12th Street for 0.2 mile, bearing left onto Finnegan Way. After 0.2 mile Finnegan merges onto 11th Street. Continue on 11th for 0.3 mile, turn left onto Bayview Drive, and drive 0.3 mile to the trailhead.

Transit: Whatcom Transit Route 401 to Fairhaven

If you've ever wanted to walk on water, the South Bay Trail is your answer. The undisputed highlight of this Bellingham Bay–hugging path is its extended offshore walkway right over the bay. From downtown, follow this sometimes soft-surface, sometimes hard-surface and always scenic section of the old Interurban Railroad to historic Fairhaven. Stop to admire points of interest, shore-probing and surf-riding birds, and

sweeping views of Bellingham Bay and Lummi Island. South
Bay Trail is one of the finest urban trails in Washington.

GET MOVING

You can access this trail from many points along its 2.5-mile
course. Parking is limited near its downtown northern terminus, but the southern terminus in Fairhaven has ample parking
nearby. Best bet is from midway at Boulevard Park (described
here) and along Bayview Drive. Boulevard Park, with its grassy
lawns, bay beaches, and concession stand, is a busy place on

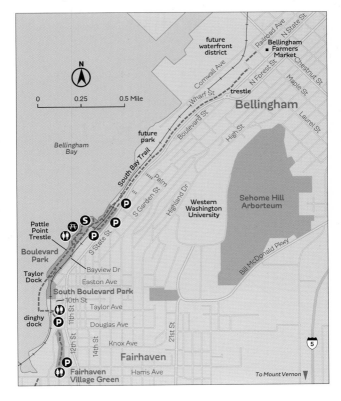

Bellingham Bay's Taylor Dock

a nice summer day. But all of those amenities also make this park a great destination for lounging *aprés* your run or walk.

The trail travels right through Boulevard Park; from there, it's 1.5 miles north to downtown and 1 mile south to Fairhaven.

If you're going to walk or run the entire trail, head north first. Pass beaches and a bandstand and a big stairway (at this writing, closed for upgrade) to the Upper Park and 14th Street. The trail, now soft-surface, cuts through a jungle of greenery along a bluff well below busy city streets. Pass interpretive signs and good views of a massive waterfront cleanup, part of which is destined to be a top-notch waterfront park. (Plan to return frequently if possible, to watch the progress—and anticipate the new running and walking opportunities.)

Pass more stairways to the roads above, providing chances to get your heart rate way up. At about 1.1 miles from the park, cross Wharf Street (use caution). Then continue on an old trestle alongside businesses and residences. The trail then ends (although not officially) on Laurel Street. To be a trail purist, follow the road left and then turn right on Railroad Avenue. Now continue on a walkway to Maple Street. Mile "0" for this trail lies just one block north. But you might not get that far, considering you are now right next to the Bellingham Farmers Market and Boundary Bay Brewery. Retrace your steps to Boulevard Park at some point.

Now head south from the park on the trail for the visual treats. Leave the happening heart of the park, emerging on the Pattle Point Trestle over a small cove. It gets better. Traverse a small patch of greenery where side paths climb the bluff above, providing excellent views of the bay. At 0.4 mile from the park, reach Taylor Dock, an extensive walkway extending over the water several hundred feet away from the shore. Enjoy the maritime bliss. Nothing can be better on a warm sunny day. Sunsets are sublime. Windy and rainy days—challenging!

The old trestle-way over water ends abruptly, but the trail continues, making a sharp left turn and climbing 75 feet or so up the bluff. This section—lined with benches for sun wor- shippers—is a great place to grind it out. Once atop the bluff, the way turns right, following quiet 10th Street (parking avail- able) a short distance before resuming soft-surface tread and ending at 1 mile near the Fairhaven Village Green. Turn around and do it all over again—perhaps diverting at 10th Street to make a side trip on the short bluff trail at neighboring South Boulevard Park.

GO FARTHER

From trail's end in Fairhaven, continue 3 blocks south along 10th Street and pick up the Interurban Trail (Trail 9). Go as far as you'd like!

2 | Bay to Baker Trail Parks

DISTANCE:	More than 6 miles of trails
ELEVATION GAIN:	Up to 150 feet
HIGH POINT:	150 feet
DIFFICULTY:	Easy
FITNESS:	Walkers, runners
FAMILY-FRIENDLY:	Yes, and stroller-friendly
DOG-FRIENDLY:	On-leash and off-leash sections
AMENITIES:	Restrooms, interpretive signs, picnic tables, play area, picnic shelter
CONTACT/MAP:	City of Bellingham Parks
GPS:	N 48° 46.029" W 122° 31.004"

GETTING THERE

Driving: *For Little Squalicum Park:* From downtown Bellingham, follow West Holly Street to Eldridge Avenue. Continue for 1.3 miles to where Eldridge becomes Marine Drive and turn right onto West Illinois Street. Then immediately turn right into the trailhead parking area. *For Squalicum Creek Park:* From downtown Bellingham, follow Roeder Avenue north for 1.3 miles. Turn right onto Squalicum Way, reaching the park in 0.6 mile. *For Cornwall Park:* From exit 256 on I-5, drive south on Meridian Street for 0.5 mile, turning left into the park.

Transit: *For Little Squalicum Park:* Whatcom Transit Route 3 to Maplewood/Cordata and Whatcom Transit Route 15 to Cordata/WCC. *For Cornwall Park:* Route 4 to Hospital/Cordata and Route 3 to Maplewood/Cordata.

The Bay to Baker Trail will eventually run all the way from Bellingham Bay to Mount Baker. Several sections of the trail are currently open, including the westernmost 1.2 miles. Utilizing an old rail bed, this short section of trail strings together three wonderful city parks, providing a host of options for adventures short and long. Each park, too, is unique. Little Squalicum Park includes a beach on Bellingham Bay. Squalicum Creek Park is one of the city's newer parks. Cornwall is one of Bellingham's oldest parks, complete with historic structures and old-growth forest.

GET MOVING

From the Little Squalicum Park Trailhead, head down a wide 0.15-mile path to the Bay to Baker Trail. Go right for 0.25 mile, crossing beneath Marine Drive and a railroad trestle and coming to Squalicum Beach. When the tide is low you can walk a short distance northwest or southeast on this Bellingham

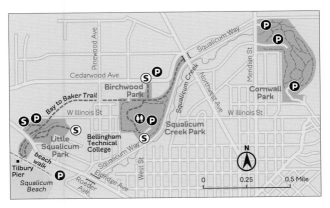

beach. This is a popular dog hangout, and your pup will love playing here. The entire Bay to Baker Trail in Little Squalicum Park is off leash.

Beyond the beach the trail makes a U-turn and heads east along the Little Squalicum Creek, reaching the Bellingham Technical College in 0.3 mile. En route, the way passes a grassy area with a short loop trail option.

Head left on the Bay to Baker Trail from the access trail and you'll soon come to West Illinois Street. Cross it and continue along some old tracks. If you have your dog with you, she needs to be leashed now. At 0.5 mile from the trailhead, cross Pinewood Avenue. At 0.7 mile, come to the edge of Squalicum Creek Park and a trail leading right. At 0.8 mile is another junction. Here a short trail leads left to Birchwood Park and a trail leads right, down a set of stairs to the loop trails within Squalicum Creek Park. You can run or walk around the park on an 0.8-mile or 1-mile loop. The trails circle busy playgrounds, sports fields, and picnic shelters. There's a large off-leash area in the park as well.

The Bay to Baker Trail continues east, passing a spur leading left to Cedarwood Avenue before reaching Squalicum Way at the Northwest Avenue bridge at 1.2 miles. Unfortunately, the trail currently doesn't continue beyond this point for some distance. You can walk or run east on Squalicum Way's wide shoulder for 0.4 mile, coming to Meridian Street and Cornwall Park.

Now explore Cornwall Park's 1.5 miles of trail, ranging from wide and paved to single track. Be sure to head over the bridges crossing Squalicum Creek above and below a little cascade at a sandstone ledge. Check out all of the old-growth giants in this park, too. The park was established in 1909 through gifts from the prominent Cornwall family. The Depression-era WPA built many of the park's historic structures. Cornwall's disc golf course is extremely popular with local college kids. The rest of the park is popular with dog walkers and runners from

Bay to Baker Trail near Squalicum Beach

all walks of life. A new 1.5-mile stretch of the Bay to Baker Trail, called the Squalicum Creek Trail, was opened in 2016. Follow this trail from Cornwall Park, passing under I-5, to reach Sunset Pond and Irongate Road.

GO FARTHER

About a half mile southeast of Little Squalicum Park is Squalicum Harbor, with its beautiful promenade walk. Access this 1.5-mile paved path around the harbor from Zuanich Park. It's a busy place, with dawdling children and sauntering couples, so don't expect a fast run. Evenings are simply divine, with the sun's fading rays dancing off of harbor waters and a shiny flotilla of watercraft.

3 Sehome Hill Arboretum

DISTANCE:	More than 6 miles of trails
ELEVATION GAIN:	Up to 350 feet
HIGH POINT:	630 feet
DIFFICULTY:	Easy to moderate
FITNESS:	Hikers, walkers, runners
FAMILY-FRIENDLY:	Yes
DOG-FRIENDLY:	On leash
AMENITIES:	Observation tower
CONTACT/MAP:	Western Washington University,
	Square One Maps: Bellingham Parks Central
GPS:	N 48° 43.680" W 122° 29.096"

GETTING THERE

Driving: From Bellingham, take exit 252 off of I-5 and drive 0.2 mile north on Samish Way. Turn left (west) onto Bill McDonald Parkway and continue for 0.9 mile. Then turn right onto 25th Street. Continue 0.1 mile, bearing right onto Arboretum Drive, immediately coming to trailhead parking on your right. Additional parking can be found at the road's end on Sehome Hill.

Transit: Whatcom Transit Route 14 to Fairhaven and Whatcom Transit Route 14S to Western Washington University.

Forming an emerald backdrop to Western Washington University (WWU), the 180-acre Sehome Hill Arboretum provides easy access to the outdoors for thousands of students and residents of area neighborhoods. Wander through mature second growth on a good complex of trails that provides plenty of loop options. If you're a runner, Sehome will provide you with a good hill workout. Just don't expect an arboretum in the sense of Seattle's Washington Park, as you won't find any manicured gardens and groves, an array of species from afar, or anything labeled. It's more like a big natural park in

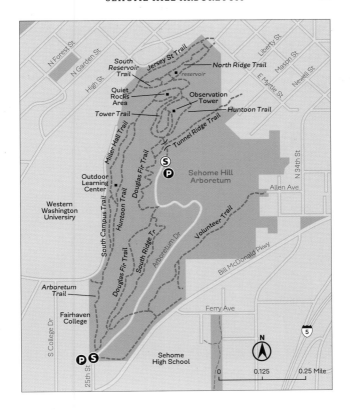

the center of Bellingham—suiting this green city's reputation just fine.

GET MOVING

The Sehome Hill Arboretum features just a few structural attractions, like the Outdoor Learning Center (benches in the woods) and an observation tower (the once-sweeping views have been lost to growing-in vegetation). These attractions and the sparse interpretive signs may be in need of updating, but the trails are regularly maintained and well used. Much of

Quiet woodland trails in the Sehome Hill Arboretum

the arboretum is closed to bicycles too, allowing for carefree strolling.

The arboretum has had a colorful past, including coal mining in the 1850s and logging in the late 1800s. In 1922 Sehome became a park. A year later, a tunnel was hand cut into a sandstone ledge on Sehome's summit for cars when they were allowed to drive over the hill. Today, you can hike through and over the tunnel—a feature young trails users will enjoy. There are several access points to the arboretum from the adjacent university and neighborhoods, so you'll see plenty of folks along the way. On some of the more quiet trails, don't be surprised if you encounter a few WWU students smoking a substance now legal in the state.

From the main parking area, the quickest way to run or hike to the summit tower (which is actually on the lower of two summit highpoints) is to take the 0.7-mile Douglas Fir Trail to the upper parking area and then walk the Tower Trail (an old road) 0.3 mile to the 80-foot wooden tower. Views north over the city to BC's Golden Ears (named for the twin peaks of Mount Blanshard) have become obscured by foliage in recent years. Loop back via the Huntoon Trail through the tunnel and then follow the Douglas Fir Trail 0.2 mile to the South Ridge Trail. Then take this quiet trail back to your start, passing over some sandstone ledges along the way. This combination makes a nice 2-mile loop with about 350 feet of elevation gain and loss.

For a somewhat longer loop, take one of the aforementioned trails to the tower then return via the Huntoon Trail north from the summit. This old road then wraps around the hill, gently descending and passing the Outdoor Learning Center, set against sandstone ledges. At 0.8 mile from the summit, bear left onto the Arboretum Trail and continue for 0.3 mile back to your start.

You can make another loop or two off of this loop by following the South Reservoir Trail from the Huntoon Trail. The old reservoir is filled in now and displays some artwork on its concrete base. Make a loop of 0.6 or 0.8 mile via the North Ridge Trail or the much nicer Jersey Street Trail, which offers views of downtown and Bellingham Bay.

Definitely walk at least atop the tunnel on the Tunnel Ridge Trail, which continues 0.3 mile downhill to Myrtle Street. The Miller Hall and South Campus Trails run parallel to the Huntoon Trail on the arboretum's west side and offer yet more loop options. The Volunteer Trail leaves the Douglas Fir Trail near the arboretum road and traverses the arboretum for 0.5 mile to Allen Avenue.

GO FARTHER

The adjacent WWU campus makes for some nice walking and running routes—especially when classes are not in session. You'll find some great stairways throughout the campus for cardio workouts. The campus is quite pretty, with its stately architecture and wide walkways, with Sehome Hill and South Hill tucked beneath.

4 Connelly Creek Trail

DISTANCE:	2 miles roundtrip
ELEVATION GAIN:	150 feet
HIGH POINT:	275 feet
DIFFICULTY:	Easy
FITNESS:	Walkers, runners
FAMILY-FRIENDLY:	Yes
DOG-FRIENDLY:	On leash
AMENITIES:	Picnic tables at Happy Valley Park
CONTACT/MAP:	City of Bellingham Parks
GPS:	N 48° 43.042" W 122° 28.702"

GETTING THERE

Driving: From Bellingham, follow I-5 south to Fairhaven exit 250. Head 0.1 mile west on Old Fairhaven Parkway and turn right onto 30th Street. Continue for 0.2 mile to the junction with Donovan Avenue and trailhead. Park at the small parking area north of the junction or along Donovan Avenue.

　　Transit: Whatcom Transit Route 105 to Fairhaven and 105S to WWU

This is a wonderful path for walkers and runners of all ages and abilities through the Connelly Creek Nature Area. Follow a good hard-surfaced path along Connelly Creek through thickets of alders, a mature cedar grove, and a patch of Sitka spruce. Spurs lead left and right to quiet neighborhood streets

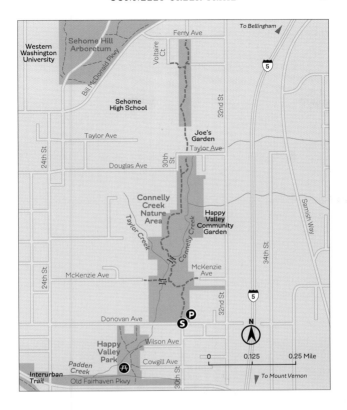

if you're looking for more exploring. A good walk or run on its own, the trail's strategic placement between the Sehome Hill Arboretum and the Interurban Trail makes it a nice connector for longer adventures.

GET MOVING

This well-groomed trail heads north through the Connelly Creek Nature Area, a linear greenbelt embracing the riparian forest of Connelly Creek and a couple of its tributaries. It's possible to push a jogging stroller on this path, although it is narrow, so be mindful of other users. The trail soon bends left where a short spur leads right to McKenzie Avenue (east). It then bends right at another junction. The spur goes straight across Connelly Creek and connects to the western section of truncated McKenzie Avenue.

The main trail then continues into a surrounding, more jungle-like forest with thick vegetation and overhanging limbs. It crosses Connelly Creek on a wooden bridge and enters a cool grove of western red cedars and Sitka spruce, a tree more common along the coastal strip. It passes a spur leading right to 32nd Street and gently ascends through mature timber. The path widens and bends left where a spur leads left through a meadow to Douglas Avenue.

At 0.6 mile you'll reach Taylor Avenue, a good turning-around spot for those interested in a short walk. Otherwise, carefully cross the street and stay on the path as it traverses Joe's Garden. In place since 1933 and resisting development pressures over the decades, this well-loved truck farm (one

Connelly Creek Trail travels through a corridor of thick vegetation.

of the few remaining farms that grows vegetables directly for markets in the Northwest) was founded by the son of Italian immigrants. You can stop and check out the organically grown produce.

The trail now enters a narrow forested strip wedged between apartments and Sehome High School and gains some elevation. A spur leads left to the high school (at Voltaire Court) before the trail ends at 1 mile at Ferry Avenue.

GO FARTHER

Extend your run or walk north by walking on Ferry Avenue two blocks west to the Bill McDonald Parkway, where you can access trails in the Sehome Hill Arboretum (Trail 3).

From the trail's southern terminus, walk 0.2 mile west on Donovan Avenue. Then head south through Happy Valley Park on a delightful 0.3-mile trail that crosses Padden Creek. You can then walk west 0.4 mile on Old Fairhaven Parkway to the Interurban Trail (Trail 9) where you can walk or run for miles.

5   Whatcom Falls

DISTANCE:	5.5 miles of trails
ELEVATION GAIN:	Up to 250 feet
HIGH POINT:	320 feet
DIFFICULTY:	Easy
FITNESS:	Walkers, runners, hikers
FAMILY-FRIENDLY:	Yes, and some trails are stroller-friendly
DOG-FRIENDLY:	On-leash and off-leash trails
AMENITIES:	Restrooms, picnic tables
CONTACT/MAP:	City of Bellingham Parks
	Square One Maps: Bellingham Parks Central
GPS:	N 48° 45.129" W 122° 25.714"

Whatcom Creek tumbles over a sandstone ledge at Whatcom Falls.

GETTING THERE

Driving: From Bellingham, follow I-5 to exit 253. Then follow Lakeway Drive east for 1.4 miles. Turn left onto Silver Beach Road and continue 0.4 mile to the trailhead. Additional parking/access is on Sunset Lane off of Electric Avenue.

   Transit: Whatcom Transit Route 11 to Geneva and 40 to Lakeway

Folks have been coming to Whatcom Falls for Sunday pic-
nics, family get-togethers, woodland strolls, and lazy summer
afternoon lounging since the 1890s. The falls on Whatcom
Creek tumbling over a sandstone ledge are beautiful. And the
forest lining the creek and its pools is attractive, offering shelter from both winter drizzle and summer heat. You can spend
an hour or all day hiking the well-maintained trails of this
241-acre park and adjacent greenbelts and trails.

GET MOVING

From the main parking area, start by taking the short paved
path down to the WPA-built sandstone arched bridge spanning Whatcom Creek below the falls. Yes, that's WPA, not WTA
(as in Washington Trails Association), as this bridge was built
in 1939–40 by the Depression-era Work Projects Administra-
tion. This FDR program, like the Civilian Conservation Corps
(CCC), helped employ millions of (mostly) young men, leaving us with a legacy of trails, roads, bridges, and parks across
the country. My paternal grandfather served in the WPA

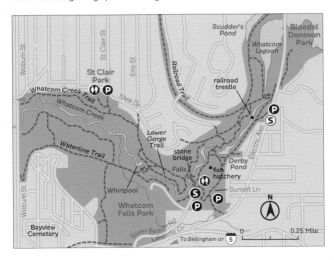

building infrastructure in New York's Bear Mountain State Park where the Appalachian Trail crosses the Hudson River. Reflect on this historic period as you explore Whatcom Falls.

After admiring Whatcom Falls—which is always a treat and especially during the wetter winter months—consider the following trail options.

WHATCOM CREEK TRAIL

This 3.1-mile trail extends from Bloedel Donovan Park on Lake Whatcom all the way to Meador Avenue just west of I-5. It then follows sidewalks, resuming in 0.6 mile to continue 0.6 mile through downtown, passing city hall and terminating at the Maritime Heritage Park near the waterfront. Except for a big section of stairs west of the Michigan Street access, the trail is jogging stroller friendly. The 0.9-mile section east of the Whatcom Falls Bridge to Bloedel Donovan Park, when combined with the trail on the south side of the creek, makes for a great nearly 2-mile loop.

From the stone bridge, head north on Whatcom Creek Trail. You'll pass some ancient trees and cross Whatcom Creek just south of the Whatcom Lagoon where the creek drains massive Lake Whatcom. Then carefully cross Electric Avenue and head to Bloedel Donovan Park, where you can go for a swim and appreciate the area's long logging and railroad history. On the return, pass an old railroad trestle, the Derby Pond (opened seasonally for children to fish), and the Fish Hatchery before returning to the trailhead.

Follow the Whatcom Creek Trail west for 1.3 miles to Woburn Street, traversing a high bluff above the cascading creek before descending a big stairway. The trail then resumes (now off the map), following alongside the creek before coming to a totem pole at 1.7 miles. The way then crosses the creek, coming to a junction with a trail leading 0.2 mile to the Salmon Woods greenbelt (see Go Farther). The Whatcom Creek Trail then continues 0.5 mile, traversing a creek

restoration area before passing beneath I-5 and coming to
Meador Avenue.

LOWER GORGE TRAIL
This wonderful little trail takes off west from the north end
of the Whatcom Falls Bridge. Follow it through big trees and
along creek rapids for 0.3 mile to a junction. Here you can
continue right to the whirlpool and then 0.1 mile farther to
its terminus with the Whatcom Creek Trail. The trail left from
the junction crosses Whatcom Creek on a high bridge and
reaches the Waterline Trail in 0.1 mile.

WATERLINE TRAIL
This wide trail is popular with cyclists and runners. It extends
for 0.7 mile from Woburn Street to the main parking lot. Use
it to make a loop with the Lower Gorge and Whatcom Creek
(via Woburn Street sidewalk) trails. The western section of
this trail is off leash. The Whatcom Falls Park Trail—another
leash-free trail—leads south from the Waterline Trail for 0.4
mile to connect with the 0.4-mile-long Lakeway Trail along
Lakeway Drive.

There are several other park trails that are generally a
little rougher, but offer more hiking and loop opportunities for
adventurous hikers and runners.

GO FARTHER
Find more trails, varying from paved to rugged, in the Salmon
Woods greenbelt and adjacent Civic Athletic Complex. From
the Whatcom Creek Trail junction you can hike the Salmon
Park Trail south for 0.8 mile, climbing out of a ravine cradling
St. Paul Creek to Lakeway Drive. Then walk east on sidewalk
and the Lakeway Trail 0.6 mile to the Whatcom Falls Park Trail
and the Waterline Trail for a loop return. And check out the
cool boardwalk paralleling Fraser Street and crossing Racine
and St. Paul creeks.

6 Railroad Trail

DISTANCE:	3.2 miles one-way
ELEVATION GAIN:	Up to 250 feet
HIGH POINT:	350 feet
DIFFICULTY:	Easy
FITNESS:	Walkers, runners
FAMILY-FRIENDLY:	Yes, and stroller friendly
DOG-FRIENDLY:	On leash
AMENITIES:	Restrooms
CONTACT/MAP:	City of Bellingham Parks
GPS:	N 48° 45.774" W 122° 25.240"

GETTING THERE

Driving: From Bellingham, follow I-5 to exit 253. Then follow Lakeway Drive east for 1.7 miles, bearing left onto Electric Avenue. Continue 1.1 miles to the trailhead (located on the left) at the junction with Alabama Street and Northshore Drive. Alternatively, you can follow Alabama Street east from downtown for 2.5 miles to the trailhead. Additional parking and an alternative start are available from Bloedel Donovan Park, 0.2 mile south on Electric Avenue. The trail can be accessed from the west, too, at Memorial Park.

Transit: Whatcom Transit Route 525 to Sunset

A wonderful linear greenbelt of more than 3 miles, the Railroad Trail threads together several city parks, from Bloedel Donovan Park on Lake Whatcom to Memorial Park. The full trail makes for a great out-and-back run of 6.4 miles—a little more than 10 kilometers, making it a great distance to train for a race. It also makes a nice walking route—particularly its eastern end, which traverses Whatcom Falls Park and the Roosevelt Nature Area. And the entire trail is stroller friendly, making it perfect for families with little ones.

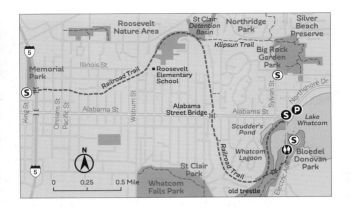

GET MOVING

On this remnant of the logging railroad that once went along Lake Whatcom (Trail 22), head west through a small field before coming to the shore of marshy Scudder's Pond, an excellent bird watching area; if you're on a run, slow your pace and check out the avian activity. Pass a side trail leading left to Whatcom Lagoon and at 0.4 mile come to a junction.

The trail left crosses Whatcom Creek on a good bridge before coming to Electric Avenue (use caution crossing) and leading to the parking area at Bloedel Donovan Park in 0.4 mile. Before the bridge, a side trail veers south to a standing section of the old trestle (built in 1916) spanning the creek. The trail heads straight to Whatcom Falls and beyond (Trail 5). You want to go right, continuing on the railroad grade, slightly ascending through an old cut.

The way soon traverses a quiet neighborhood, crossing a couple of lightly traveled streets and passing a few short spurs leading to other roads. At 1 mile, come to the Alabama Street Bridge. Definitely pause on this span across the busy roadway below. Positioned on a hillside, the bridge grants a sweeping view west across the city to Sehome Hill and the San Juan Islands.

The Railroad Trail passing by old trestle remnants

The trail then continues through a forested corridor on a slight descent, passing more side trails to neighborhood streets. Enjoy a pleasant run or walk, meeting folks of all ages and backgrounds along the way. At 1.6 miles, come to a junction with the Klipsun Trail (Trail 7), which can be used to make a good loop, complete with hill and step workout.

The Railroad Trail bends west, passing the St. Clair Detention Basin and the Roosevelt Nature Area, two little greenbelts usually bustling with birds. Pass through a row of old trestle supports and skirt around busy Barkley Village (with several cafes and restaurants that may lure you from the trail) before reaching Woburn Street at 2.2 miles. This is a good spot to turn around, as beyond the trail the surroundings become more urban and less scenic.

If you continue, carefully cross Woburn Street and follow the trail mostly through neighborhoods and light industrial areas, eventually crossing humming I-5 and ending at Memorial Park, which honors Whatcom County residents who gave their lives in battle for their country. There are restrooms in the park.

You can alternatively start your Railroad Trail workout from this location on King Street, two blocks north of Alabama Street.

GO FARTHER

Combine the Railroad Trail with the Klipsun Trail or trails within Whatcom Falls Park (see trails 5 and 7) for longer runs and walks of varying distances.

7 | Klipsun Trail and Northridge Park

DISTANCE:	3.2 miles of trails
ELEVATION GAIN:	Up to 350 feet
HIGH POINT:	575 feet
DIFFICULTY:	Easy to moderate
FITNESS:	Walkers, runners
FAMILY-FRIENDLY:	Yes
DOG-FRIENDLY:	On leash
AMENITIES:	Restrooms
CONTACT/MAP:	City of Bellingham Parks
GPS:	N 48° 46.147" W 122° 25.257"

GETTING THERE

Driving: From Bellingham, follow I-5 to exit 253. Then follow Lakeway Drive east for 1.7 miles, bearing left onto Electric

Avenue. Continue 1.1 miles to the junction with Alabama Street and Northshore Drive (alternatively, you can follow Alabama Street east from downtown for 2.5 miles). Turn left onto Alabama Street, then immediately turn right onto Sylvan Street. Continue north for 0.4 mile, turning right onto Balsam Lane. Continue for 0.1 mile to the trailhead at Big Rock Garden Park.

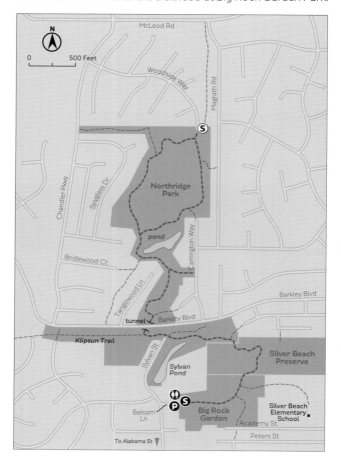

Transit: Whatcom Transit Route 525 to Sunset stops on Alabama Street. Walk on Sylvan Street to the trailhead.

If you are looking to get your heart rate up, you'll love the Klipsun Trail. Starting from Big Rock Garden Park on a forested hilltop, you can only go downhill—requiring an uphill return. Choose a graded incline, one with steps, or both. Adjoining Northridge Park offers a mellower trail system, with a hilltop loop through big trees and around a small wetland pool.

GET MOVING

Before or after your workout—and especially if this is your first time at Big Rock Garden Park—absolutely allot some time for a stroll through the 2.5-acre garden (pets prohibited). Here paths weave through sculptures and manicured grounds and a Japanese garden that boasts more than 100 varieties of maples—purely spectacular in the fall. The rhododendrons make a spring visit a must.

From the garden, follow the Klipsun Trail, soon coming to a junction. The short path right (south) leads downhill, terminating on Peters Street. Here you can walk a couple of blocks south to pick up the Railroad Trail (Trail 6). Continue left and soon come to another junction. The trail to the right leads downhill through the Silver Beach Preserve, a 22-acre forested tract once slated for fifty-seven home sites. This spur ends at the Silver Beach Elementary School.

The Klipsun Trail continues left (north). Ignore a spur heading right to a subdivision and continue left on a rougher track (not suitable for strollers) skirting Sylvan Pond through mature forest. The way soon becomes wider and better groomed. At 0.6 mile, come to a junction. The trail right leads through a tunnel (that kids will love) beneath Barkley Boulevard, entering Northridge Park.

Get a good step workout on the Klipsun Trail.

This nice little hilltop park in the Mount Baker neighborhood is primarily used by area residents. Follow the trail north for 0.2 mile, passing a small duck pond, to a 0.7-mile loop through mature woods. The wide trail is stroller friendly. Several spurs radiate out from it, including a 0.2-mile trail to Chandler Parkway and a 0.3-mile trail to McLeod Road near Squalicum High School.

Return to the Klipsun Trail and continue west through a patch of forest; the trail next drops more than 300 feet via a series of steps. This is a great area to do some hill climb intervals for strength training. On your way to the steps, look for an enormous cottonwood towering over the trail. At 1.2 miles from Big Rock Garden Park, reach the Railroad Trail near the St. Clair Detention Basin. Turn around or consider the loop that follows.

GO FARTHER

Turning left, follow the Railroad Trail south for 1.6 miles to its trailhead. Then walk north on Dakin Street for three blocks, turning right on Silver Beach Avenue. After one block, walk left on Peters Street, pick up the Klipsun Trail and follow it 0.25 mile back to your start. In case you're wondering, *klipsun* is Chinook jargon for sunset—and you may catch some good ones from the Alabama Street bridge on the Railroad Trail.

8 Lake Padden Park

DISTANCE:	More than 9 miles of trails
ELEVATION GAIN:	Up to 600 feet
HIGH POINT:	940 feet
DIFFICULTY:	Easy to moderate
FITNESS:	Hikers, walkers, runners
FAMILY-FRIENDLY:	Yes, and Lake Loop Trail and Padden Gorge Trail are suitable for jogging strollers

DOG-FRIENDLY: On-leash and off-leash trails
AMENITIES: Picnic tables, privy
CONTACT/MAP: City of Bellingham Parks
Square One Maps: Chuckanut Recreation Area
GPS: N 48° 42.346" W 122° 27.405"

GETTING THERE

Driving: From Bellingham, follow I-5 south to Fairhaven exit 252. Continue south on Samish Way for 2.3 miles, turning right into the beach access area and parking. From Mount Vernon, head north on I-5 to exit 246. Then follow Samish Way north for 2.8 miles, turning left into the park. Alternative parking and trailheads can be found on Lakeshore Drive (0.3 mile east on Lake Samish Way from the beach access) and on Samish Way 1.5 miles east of the beach access entrance.

Transit: Whatcom Transit Route 43 to Yew Street A.M.; Whatcom Transit Route 44 to Yew Street P.M.

In a city with many recreational gems, Lake Padden is one of Bellingham's crown jewels. The 160-acre lake once served as the city's water supply. In 1968 it was transferred to the parks

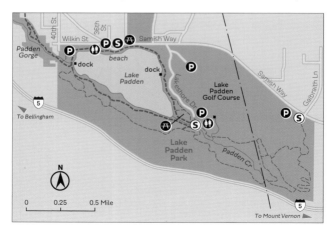

View of Lookout Mountain across Lake Padden from the dock at the lake's outlet

department, where it has been expanded to include more than 1000 acres. The undeveloped lake is surrounded by ancient timber and flanked by emerald hills, making it feel like it's deep in the hinterlands. But it's a mere few miles from downtown. An extensive trail system here, however, keeps crowding down and allows for a lot of exploring for hikers, walkers, and runners.

GET MOVING

The most popular trail at Lake Padden—and one you definitely want to take if you have never visited here—is the 2.7-mile loop trail. This wide, well-groomed path can be accessed from several of the park's parking areas. It loops around the lake, passing through groves of mature conifers and along beaches and quiet coves. All but along the southern shoreline, where the trail becomes rolling, the way is nearly level. This path is ideal for hikers, walkers, and runners of all ages and abilities. You won't have too much trouble pushing a jogging stroller on it.

From the lake's southeast corner near its inlet creek, you can set off on 4 miles of off-leash trails. You can access these trails from the Lake Loop, the parking area at the end of Lakeshore Drive (near the dog park), or the eastern trailhead on Samish Way. These trails are popular with trail runners and their unleashed four-legged companions, and they're quite a bit more rugged than the popular loop and Padden Gorge trails. The off-leash trails loop around Padden Creek and include a few knolls, including the highest point in the park (elev. 940 feet).

Just to the west of the off-leash trails is a trail that runs parallel with the loop trail's southern shore section. If you want some variation from the Lake Loop, veer onto this trail (which mainly follows an old road). This trail will give you not only a little extra mileage, but also some hill work as it travels along a small ridge, dipping in and out of ravines. A couple of short trails veer right from it, leading back to the lake loop; you can make a few loops here—perhaps giving your trail run some nice hill work.

At the lake's outlet is a dock where you can enjoy gorgeous views of Lookout Mountain across the lake—and find the Padden Gorge Trail. This wonderful, wide, well-groomed trail follows Padden Creek from the old lake dam through an emerald gorge, passing big trees and old stone structures. The trail ends at 36th Street (no parking) after a half mile and dropping about 125 feet. There is a small loop you can follow on your return. In the fall and winter after some rainfall this trail is exceptionally appealing, as Padden Creek tumbles and cascades through the gorge.

GO FARTHER

From the Padden Gorge Trail's end at 36th Street, you can walk a short distance on that road to a short trail taking you to 34th Street. Then follow 34th Street two blocks north to Old Fairhaven Parkway, where you can walk about 0.6 mile west to the Interurban Trail (Trail 9).

Next page: *Lummi Island from Clayton Beach*

CHUCKANUT MOUNTAINS

The only place where the Cascades meet the Salish Sea, the Chuckanuts offer a wonderful mix of low mountain and coastal landscapes. Forming a greenbelt between the growing Mount Vernon and Bellingham municipalities, the Chuckanuts provide important wildlife habitat and excellent recreation opportunities. Much of the range is contained within county parks as well as state park, state forest, and state fish and wildlife lands. More than 9000 acres of public land here are managed for wildlife, timber production, and outdoor recreation. An excellent network of interconnecting trails traverses nearly the entire range and connects the Chuckanuts to Bellingham. In these gentle mountains of folded sandstone, explore small, quiet lakes, ledges providing breathtaking panoramas, secluded coastal coves, and pockets of old-growth forest.

9 Interurban Trail

DISTANCE:	6.6 miles one-way, with miles of side trips
ELEVATION GAIN:	Up to 950 feet
HIGH POINT:	500 feet
DIFFICULTY:	Easy to moderate
FITNESS:	Hikers, walkers, runners,
FAMILY-FRIENDLY:	All but the Arroyo Park section is jogging stroller friendly
DOG-FRIENDLY:	On leash
AMENITIES:	Privy and water at Fairhaven Park and Larrabee State Park
CONTACT/MAP:	City of Bellingham Parks, Square One Maps: Chuckanut Recreation Area
GPS:	N 48° 42.862" W 122° 29.840"

GETTING THERE

Driving: From Bellingham, follow I-5 south (from Mount Vernon, follow I-5 north) to Fairhaven exit 250. Then head 1.3 miles west on Old Fairhaven Parkway (State Route 11) and turn left onto 12th Street (still SR 11). Continue south for 0.2 mile and turn left into Fairhaven Park for trailhead parking.

The northernmost 6.6-mile segment of an old trolley line that linked Bellingham to Mount Vernon from 1912 to 1930 is now a popular multi-use trail stringing together an emerald necklace of parks and greenbelts. Stroll for an hour or spend all day running this wide path and its radiating trails. Visit a historic district, historic farm, old-growth forests, waterfalls, placid pond, quiet estuary, remote cove, and viewpoints granting sweeping vistas all from this one trail and a handful of its spurs.

GET MOVING

The trail officially begins at 10th Street in the historic Fairhaven District and ends in Larrabee State Park. Parking is limited at its northern terminus in Fairhaven, making nearby Fairhaven Park, with its large parking area and restroom facilities, a better starting point. The trail's southern terminus at Larrabee State Park offers ample parking (a Discover Pass is required) and privies. There are many other trail access parking areas along the way, allowing you to sample the trail at various locations. What follows is a brief description of the

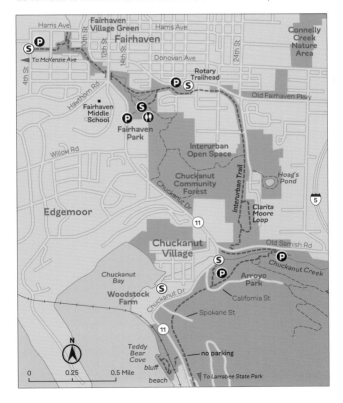

trail and some of its side trails. Have fun creating your own adventures—and plan to return often.

Starting from the beautiful 1906-established Fairhaven Park, three short trails access the Interurban Trail. To head northbound on the Interurban, locate a connector trail at the rear of the park's pavilion. Cross Padden Creek in a wooded ravine and reach the Interurban Trail. Here a spur also leads north 0.1 mile to 14th Street. Note a milepost denoting "3." The Interurban is marked with half-mile posts that actually begin at the start of the South Bay Trail (also part of an old rail line) in downtown Bellingham.

Now turn left and follow the creek downstream, passing under the 12th Street Bridge. At about 0.3 mile the trail pops up on 10th Street. Here you can walk a couple of blocks north through the Victorian-era Fairhaven District (once a separate city from Bellingham) and continue on the South Bay Trail (Trail 1), or continue on the connecting Larrabee (Lower Padden Creek) Trail. Follow along the creek for a short distance, then cross it where spurs lead north to Harris Avenue and east to 8th Street. The Larrabee Trail then reaches 4th Street (parking available) at 0.7 mile.

From there you can continue farther west on the 4th Street Loop Trail, which circles around the water treatment plant for 0.4 mile to McKenzie Avenue. The western half of this loop includes an off-leash area. The eastern half of the loop passes an observation deck for the small but bird-rich Post Point Estuary. The treatment plant features some architecture you might find intriguing.

To travel southbound on the Interurban Trail from Fairhaven Park, take the spur trail near the tennis courts. After 0.1 mile, reach the Interurban and start heading right. At about 0.3 mile, come to the recently daylighted section of Padden Creek. Here a bridge spans the creek to the Rotary Trailhead located on the Old Fairhaven Parkway.

Teddy Bear Cove

The Interurban continues by some apartment complexes and crosses several quiet streets. At 0.5 mile it bends south near 24th Street. From here you can veer left and walk 0.2 mile on sidewalk along the Old Fairhaven Parkway, picking up the Happy Valley Park Trail leading to the Connelly Creek Trail (Trail 4).

The Interurban now makes a straight, level cut through a tunnel of hawthorns. At 1 mile, come to a junction. Here you can head left for a 0.6-mile cherry stem loop to and around peaceful Hoag's Pond. Bring your binoculars for birding. You can head right here on an unmarked trail into the Chuckanut Community Forest, also known as the Hundred Acre Wood. Here a maze of unmarked trails leads up over a 280-foot wooded hill and to trailheads on Chuckanut Drive and back to Fairhaven Park. You can easily get lost in here—which can be either fun or frustrating. If you can negotiate the trail complex, it's about 1.2 miles back to Fairhaven Park.

The Interurban continues south through a peaceful wooded tract, soon coming to another junction. Here the Clarita Moore Trail takes off left, climbing to a small ridge sporting big cedars before dropping and returning to the Interurban in 0.3 mile. This makes a nice diversion; otherwise continue south and begin switchbacking down to Old Samish Road (no parking here) at 1.5 miles. Carefully cross the road and drop into a ravine of attractive old growth. The old trestle here over Chuckanut Creek is long gone, requiring a pretty— but not stroller friendly—route across the Chuckanut Creek gorge in Arroyo Park.

The way climbs out of the gorge and passes two trails heading left to a myriad of trails in the Chuckanut Mountains (see trails 10, 11, 12, 14, and 15). Pass a little waterfall, coming to a junction at 2.3 miles. Here a spur leads to the right 0.2 mile to the North Chuckanut Mountain Trailhead—a starting point for many adventures in the Chuckanut Mountains and a good starting point for exploring Teddy Bear Cove.

The Interurban Trail crosses California Street, makes a steep climb, then follows a right-of-way for a handful of residences. At 2.5 miles the trail comes to quiet Spokane Street. Here you can walk right 0.1 mile—carefully cross Chuckanut Drive and explore the city of Bellingham's historic Woodstock Farm (reachable by car; limited parking).

The former estate of Vermont transplant Cyrus Lester Gates, a prominent local parks and public works leader and philanthropist, Woodstock Farm was built between 1905 and 1925. It was named for Woodstock, Vermont, the home of George Perkins Marsh, considered the country's first conservationist. Gates's legacy includes his role in helping to create Larrabee State Park, Arroyo Park, and Fairhaven Park. Wander the manicured grounds and the farm's 0.5-mile and 0.3-mile loops. Enjoy gorgeous views of Chuckanut Bay and check out some of the big ornamental trees growing on the premises.

The Interurban Trail continues south, reaching another junction at 2.6 miles. Here you can head right, carefully cross Chuckanut Drive (note: no parking at this trailhead), and then hike 0.3 mile, steeply descending 225 feet via switchbacks and stairs to Teddy Bear Cove. Be extremely careful crossing the active railroad tracks just before the cove. Enjoy exploring the tide pools and sandstone ledges at this favorite local coastal spot. Notice rare Garry oaks growing on the bluff above the rocky beach.

The Interurban Trail then follows a private road for a short distance and resumes on a wide, soft-surface trail suitable for jogging strollers. It traverses steep, forested slopes high above Chuckanut Bay, passing several openings that offer sweeping views over the sparkling, island-dotted waters below. Pass a few cascading creeks too. At 4.6 miles, cross Hiline Road (trailhead parking), which becomes Cleator Road as it enters Larrabee State Park.

Now drop into a ravine—thanks to a missing trestle—and make the steep climb out. Continue traversing woodlands and a couple of private drives before entering Larrabee State Park at about 5.3 miles. The trail then goes through some cool grade cuts and passes the popular Fragrance Lake Trail (Trail 13) and a spur leading to the Lost Lake Trailhead (parking and restrooms), that soon terminates at 6.2 miles on Chuckanut Drive (State Route 11).

10 Arroyo Park and Chuckanut Falls

DISTANCE:	2 miles roundtrip
ELEVATION GAIN:	450 feet
HIGH POINT:	350 feet
DIFFICULTY:	Moderate
FITNESS:	Hikers, runners
FAMILY-FRIENDLY:	Yes, but trails also open to bikes; sections can be muddy in winter
DOG-FRIENDLY:	Off leash under control in Arroyo Park; on leash in county park
AMENITIES:	Benches
CONTACT/MAP:	City of Bellingham Parks, Square One Maps: Chuckanut Recreation Area
GPS:	N 48° 42.147" W 122° 28.857"

GETTING THERE

Driving: From Bellingham, follow I-5 south to Fairhaven exit 250. Head 0.1 mile west on Old Fairhaven Parkway and turn left onto 30th Street. Continue for 1 mile (the road becomes 32nd Street), turning right onto Old Samish Road. Proceed for 0.2 mile to the trailhead and parking on the left.

From Mount Vernon, follow I-5 north to exit 246 and drive west on Old Samish Road for 4.2 miles to the park trailhead and parking on your left. Additional parking can be found a little farther west and at the North Chuckanut Mountain Trailhead (alternative start).

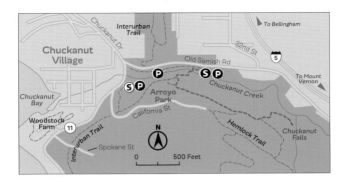

Arroyo Park is a regular Grand Central Station of trails. A lot of adventures begin from this natural area just south of Bellingham's historic Fairhaven District. The trip to Chuckanut Falls is perfect for hikers young and old, and it can be made after school or work. While the small falls are lovely, it's the big trees along the way that deserve much of your admiration.

GET MOVING

Established in 1923 with a 38-acre gift from Vermont transplant and Bellingham civic leader Cyrus Gates, Arroyo Park contains some of Bellingham's oldest and grandest trees. From the trailhead, drop into the "arroyo" carved by tumbling Chuckanut Creek. The term "arroyo" usually refers to a wash, dry creek bed, or gulch that temporarily flows, usually after a heavy rainfall. They are typically found throughout the arid American Southwest. Here, though, is a lush, green ravine with a robust year-round creek.

At 0.1 mile, come to a junction with the Interurban Trail (Trail 9) at an attractive bridge. The way right goes to the alternative parking on Old Samish Road and beyond to Fairhaven. This adventure requires a left turn over the bridge; then begin climbing out of the ravine. A few switchbacks help ease the grade. At 0.2 mile, reach a signed junction. The Interurban

Trail continues straight, crossing California Creek below a pretty cascade before coming to a junction in 0.3 mile. Here the way right leads 0.2 mile to the North Chuckanut Mountain Trailhead—an alternative starting point for this trip.

At the signed junction, veer left, climbing through a grove of conifers impressive in their size, girth, and age. Bear left at an unmarked junction (the trail right leads to the Interurban Trail) and continue gaining elevation, passing more majestic trees and a giant glacial erratic along the way.

At 0.7 mile, reach a junction (elev. 350 feet). Now in county parkland (where your four-legged friend needs to be on leash) and second growth, bear left; the way right leads to the Hemlock Trail. Soon come to another junction (the way right also leads to the Hemlock Trail). Go left, gently descending through a grove of big maples and reaching the trail's end (elev. 225 feet) at the falls. Here you can sit on a bench and admire the small 30-foot or so waterfall tumbling over a sandstone ledge. Return the way you came or combine with other trips in the Chuckanut Recreation Area.

GO FARTHER

Two more family-friendly, fairly easy adventures can be made from either the Arroyo Park Trailhead (APT) or the North Chuckanut Mountain Trailhead (NCMT). Continue south on the Interurban Trail, crossing California Street and reaching Spokane Street 0.6 mile from the NCMT or 0.9 mile from the APT. Here walk right 0.1 mile on Spokane Street and then carefully cross Chuckanut Drive (State Route 11), coming to Woodstock Farm. The historic 1905 farm, now owned by the city, was once the home of Cyrus Gates, who was responsible for establishing several Bellingham parks. Visit the farm grounds on Chuckanut Bay via a 0.6-mile trail.

For the second adventure, continue south on the Interurban Trail for another 0.2 mile to a junction. Turn left here and descend stairs before carefully crossing Chuckanut Drive

Chuckanut Falls

(SR 11). Then continue on the trail and stairway, dropping 225 feet in 0.3 mile, to beautiful Teddy Bear Cove on Chuckanut Bay. Use extreme caution crossing the railroad tracks just before the beach. Enjoy wandering the beach or basking on the scenic shoreline.

11   Pine and Cedar Lakes

DISTANCE:	5.2 miles roundtrip
ELEVATION GAIN:	1625 feet
HIGH POINT:	1825 feet
DIFFICULTY:	Difficult
FITNESS:	Hikers, runners
FAMILY-FRIENDLY:	Yes, but some trails also open to bikes and horses; the trail may be too steep for most young children
DOG-FRIENDLY:	On leash
AMENITIES:	Privy, backcountry campsites
CONTACT/MAP:	Whatcom County Parks and Recreation, Washington Fish and Wildlife, Square One Maps: Chuckanut Recreation Area
GPS:	N 48° 41.436" W 122° 27.193"

GETTING THERE

Driving: From Bellingham, follow I-5 south to Fairhaven exit 250. Head 0.1 mile west on Old Fairhaven Parkway and turn left onto 30th Street. Continue for 1 mile (the road becomes 32nd Street), turning left onto Old Samish Road. Proceed for 1.3 miles to the trailhead on your right.

From Mount Vernon, follow I-5 north to exit 246 (North Lake Samish). Turn right; cross the freeway and in 0.3 mile turn right onto Old Samish Road. Proceed for 2.7 miles to the trailhead on your left. A privy is available.

Don't let the short distance to these two little lakes tucked high on Chuckanut Mountain fool you. You'll get a good work-out in getting to them, thanks to the steep initial approach. But once you conquer that climb—heart rate up and fully limber—enjoy exploring the lakes and a knob above them with some pretty decent views.

GET MOVING

The trails to Pine and Cedar lakes traverse a patchwork of public lands containing the sprawling Chuckanut Mountains Trail System, weaving together City of Bellingham parks, Whatcom County parks, Washington State parks, and Department of Fish and Wildlife lands. You'll hardly notice any change in ownership, as the abutting agencies have agreed to manage these tracts in a like fashion: undeveloped and for nonmotorized recreation and wildlife enhancement.

The entire way is through deep, unbroken forest. Most of it is second growth, but there are some ancient trees here and there. And while the buzz of vehicles zipping along nearby I-5 reminds you just how close to civilization you really are, much of the way feels remote. Starting at an elevation just

Placid Pine Lake

below 300 feet, head up the steep trail under a canopy of maturing hemlock, cedar, and maple. The trail, an old skid road, passes rushing creeks, pocket wetlands, and a few patches of big old trees.

In about 0.7 mile the trail angles left, leaving the old road and now taking a more gradual approach toward its destinations. At 1.6 miles, crest a slope at 1600 feet, and come to a junction with the Hemlock Trail. A right turn heads toward Raptor Ridge (Trail 12) and the North Chuckanut Mountain Trailhead. You want to go left, on a former logging railroad grade, now a wide, pleasant path. Pass an unmarked trail on your left—your return route. Continue straight, entering a notched valley. Lose the I-5 hum and begin concentrating, in season, on the melodies of thrushes, warblers, and flycatchers.

At 1.8 miles, come to a junction (elev. 1650 feet). Left leads to Cedar Lake. Head right first, to Pine Lake, passing another trail leading left to Cedar Lake. Follow an up-and-down trail along a narrow fold, reaching Pine Lake (elev. 1600 feet) at 2.1 miles. Here narrow boardwalks lead several hundred feet left and right across lakeshore wetlands to backcountry campsites. Yes, you can spend the night here if you'd like. The two sites—particularly the one to the left, on a small peninsula—make nice lunch spots too. You're surrounded by cedars; the only pine here seems to be the lake's name.

Now retrace your steps 0.3 mile back to either of the trails leading right to Cedar Lake. Take one of them and drop about 50 vertical feet, reaching the lake in 0.2 mile. A good trail circles the small lake surrounded by cedars, Douglas firs, and a couple of Sitka spruce (more common on the Olympic coast). The complete loop is 0.4 mile. On the lake's western shore is a nice clearing. And here a trail takes off to climb the 1825-foot nearby knoll.

Take it, steeply climbing through attractive, mature forest. Pass two good viewpoints before reaching the summit and a good viewpoint on a precipitous ledge at 0.5 mile. Enjoy the view of Mount Baker and Lookout Mountain. Then continue, soon coming to another viewpoint—this one west to Lummi Island. The trail then switchbacks downward, reaching a familiar junction in 0.4 mile. Turn right and bear right soon afterward—then enjoy a 1.6-mile downhill jaunt to your start.

GO FARTHER

Pine and Cedar lakes can also be accessed via the Hemlock Trail from the North Chuckanut Mountain Trailhead. This route to the Pine and Cedar lakes junction is about 4.2 miles long. Add a few extra hundred feet of elevation gain, too. From the Hemlock–Pine and Cedar lakes junction it's 0.6 mile to the Raptor Ridge trail. The way is fairly gentle, passing through a sandstone notch.

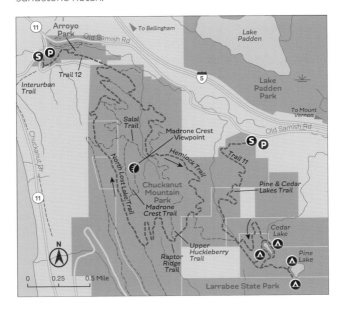

12   Raptor Ridge

DISTANCE:	8.3 miles roundtrip
ELEVATION GAIN:	1700 feet
HIGH POINT:	1630 feet
DIFFICULTY:	Moderate
FITNESS:	Hikers, runners
FAMILY-FRIENDLY:	Yes, but some trails also open to mountain bikes and horses; use caution at the viewpoint
DOG-FRIENDLY:	On leash
AMENITIES:	Benches
CONTACT/MAP:	Whatcom County Parks and Recreation Square One Maps: Chuckanut Recreation Area
GPS:	N 48° 42.088" W 122° 29.348"

GETTING THERE

Driving: From Bellingham, follow I-5 south to Fairhaven exit 250. Head 0.1 mile west on Old Fairhaven Parkway and turn left onto 30th Street. Continue for 1 mile (the road becomes 32nd Street), turning right onto Old Samish Road. Then proceed for 0.6 mile, bearing left onto Chuckanut Drive (State Route 11). Reach the trailhead in 0.1 mile.

From Mount Vernon, follow I-5 north to exit 246 (North Lake Samish) and drive west on Old Samish Road for 4.6 miles, bearing left onto Chuckanut Drive; the trailhead is 0.1 mile farther.

You'll burn some calories running or hiking to this fairly lonely ridge in the heart of the Chuckanut Recreation Area. Built primarily by volunteers with mountain biking organizations, much of the trail is, as bikers like to say, flowy. It makes for great trail running and relaxing hiking. There are some interesting ledges along the way, including one that affords a pretty darn good view down Oyster Creek and out to Blanchard Mountain.

GET MOVING

From the busy North Chuckanut Mountain Trailhead (elev. 60 feet), follow the trail 0.2 mile to the Interurban Trail. Then turn left, cross a cascading creek, and reach a junction at 0.5 mile. Head right, climbing through a beautiful old-growth grove, reaching a junction at 1 mile. You'll be returning right, so continue straight. Then bear right at the next junction, where a trail leads left to Chuckanut Falls (Trail 10). At 1.5 miles, reach a junction with the Hemlock Trail.

Now follow this trail—an old logging road—left, crossing a creek and steadily climbing. At 2.2 miles the Huckleberry Trail heads left. At 2.6 miles, come to a major intersection (elev. 1000 feet). Here the Salal Trail takes off right to reach the North Lost Lake Trail in 0.5 mile, offering a shortcut. The Huckleberry Trail leads north here, returning to the Hemlock Trail in 0.8 mile and passing a viewpoint that's being lost to encroaching vegetation. The Upper Huckleberry Trail heads right (see Go Farther), reaching the Raptor Ridge Trail in 1.1 miles and offering another loop option.

Continue left on the Hemlock Trail for a gentle ascent, coming to the Raptor Ridge Trail (elev. 1450 feet) at 3.6 miles. The Hemlock Trail continues left and east through a sand-stone notch, reaching the Pine and Cedar Lakes Trail in 0.6 mile, an alternative approach to Raptor Ridge.

The Raptor Ridge Trail leads right, soon heading upward (aided by steps) past impressive overhanging sandstone ledges. At 3.9 miles, come to an open sandstone outcropping (elev. 1630 feet). Exercise caution here and enjoy the good view down the Oyster Creek valley and out to Blanchard Mountain and beyond. Then continue hiking, coming to a junction (elev. 1500 feet) at 4 miles. Here the fairly new and well-constructed Upper Huckleberry Trail takes off right, returning to the Hemlock Trail.

The Raptor Ridge Trail continues left, wrapping around the ridge and passing beneath more ledges. It then crosses a tight

Blanchard Mountain and the Oyster Creek Valley from Raptor Ridge

notch and wraps around another ridge before descending on a long, gentle switchback. Finally it passes wetlands, reaching the North Lost Lake Trail (elev. 1250 feet) at 4.9 miles.

Now turn right (north) and follow this trail—an old road. At 5.4 miles, pass the Madrone Crest Trail. At 5.9 miles, come to a junction with the Lower Chuckanut Ridge and Salal trails.

Continue straight on the North Lost Lake Trail and begin a long descent. Pass the Lower Salal Trail and come to the Hemlock Trail at 6.9 miles. Turn left (soon bearing right at a junction with a path leading to California Street) and reach a familiar junction at 7.3 miles. Head left here and return to your start at 8.3 miles.

GO FARTHER

You can extend this hike with a trip to Lost Lake (add 4 miles roundtrip), a trip to Pine and Cedar lakes (add 2.6 miles roundtrip), or a trip to Chuckanut Falls (add 0.6 mile roundtrip). If you take the Huckleberry Trail, it'll add 0.4 mile to the loop and bring you to a limited viewpoint north. The Upper Huckleberry Trail heads 1.1 miles up and over Raptor Ridge (elev. 1575 feet) before descending to the Raptor Ridge Trail; from there, it is 0.1 mile left to the viewpoint. This makes for a shorter trip than continuing on the Hemlock Trail.

You can add a side trip (1 mile roundtrip and 200 feet elevation gain) to the Madrone Crest Viewpoint. Note: This viewpoint is also getting grown in and is not too expansive. The Lower Salal Trail is a twisty, banked trail only a mountain biker would love, but the Salal Trail is a nice hike and can be used with the Madrone Crest Trail for some variation from the North Lost Lake Trail—also adding a little extra distance.

13   Fragrance Lake

DISTANCE:	4.4 miles roundtrip
ELEVATION GAIN:	1050 feet
HIGH POINT:	1100 feet
DIFFICULTY:	Moderate
FITNESS:	Hikers, runners

FAMILY-FRIENDLY:	Yes, but trail is steep in places
DOG-FRIENDLY:	On leash
AMENITIES:	Benches, privy
CONTACT/MAP:	Washington State Parks
	Square One Maps: Chuckanut Recreation Area
GPS:	N 48° 39.200" W 122° 29.410"
BEFORE YOU GO:	A Discover Pass is required.

GETTING THERE

Driving: From Bellingham, follow I-5 south to Fairhaven exit 250. Head 0.1 mile west on Old Fairhaven Parkway and turn left onto 30th Street. Continue for 1 mile (the road becomes 32nd Street), turning right onto Old Samish Road. Then proceed for 0.6 mile, bearing left onto Chuckanut Drive (State Route 11). Continue 4 miles south to the trailhead (elev. 140 feet) located near the Larrabee State Park Campground entrance

From Mount Vernon, head north on I-5 to exit 231. Then follow SR 11 (Chuckanut Drive) north for 14.6 miles to the trailhead just beyond the Lost Lake Trailhead. Alternative parking is located near the campground entrance booth and at Lost Lake Trailhead.

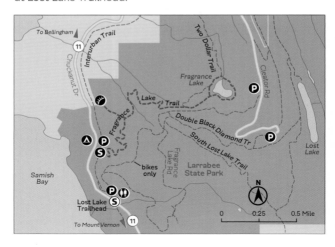

Perhaps the most popular spot in the Chuckanut Mountains, Fragrance Lake sees legions of hikers and runners old and young and of all shapes and sizes. Follow a foot traffic–only trail, steeply at times, through groves of big old-growth trees to the small placid lake—the gem of Larrabee State Park. Then amble around it, passing babbling brooks, big cedars, and steep sandstone ledges. And be sure to take the side trip along the way to a scenic overlook of glistening Samish Bay dotted with emerald islands.

GET MOVING

Folks have been hiking here for over a century. Larrabee State Park was established in 1915 as Washington's first state park through a gift from Frances Larrabee. Her husband, Xavier, was quite an entrepreneur and founder of Fairhaven. Frances was quite a philanthropist and particularly involved with children's issues. Her initial gift to the state of 20 acres upon her husband's death was followed shortly afterward with 1500 more acres. Today, Larrabee State Park consists of more than 2600 acres traversed by 15 miles of trails.

The Fragrance Lake trail commences in a series of short steep switchbacks. Waste no time warming up. Upward mobility is quickly interrupted, however, upon intersecting the Interurban Trail (see Trail 9). Once a trolley line that serviced Mount Vernon and Bellingham in the early 20th century, the rail bed was converted into a 6.6-mile trail in the late 1980s.

Cross the Interurban Trail, regaining the Fragrance Lake Trail a few dozen feet to your right. Pass through a stile meant to keep errant mountain bikers out. Then the trail winds its way upward through a dark, dank forest of mature western cedar, noble fir, and Douglas fir. At 0.7 mile (elev. 600 feet), reach a well-marked junction. Take the fairly level side path 0.2 mile left to a madrona-framed ledge granting delightful views westward over Samish Bay to Cypress, Vendovi, Sinclair, and Lummi islands.

Soak up the scenery and perhaps some sunshine and return 0.2 mile to the junction. Then head left, briefly dipping into a damp ravine and skirting a small creek. The way then climbs steeply under a thick green canopy. At 1.9 miles, pass through another bike barricade and arrive at another junction (elev. 1100 feet). The trail right leads to an old road and more hiking options (see Go Farther). The trail left heads to Fragrance Lake—take it.

Passing mossy cedars and big stumps of the old-growth trees that once grew here, slightly descend into a muddy depression. At 2.1 miles, reach a junction at Fragrance Lake (elev. 1050 feet). Here a 0.6-mile trail loops around the lake. Take it, passing a couple of shoreline benches and big cedars. Admire babbling brooks along the eastern shore and a series of sandstone ledges along the western shore. Stay for awhile and return the way you came or consider the options that follow.

GO FARTHER

For a slightly longer return and one easier on your knees, take the gated Fragrance Lake Road right. In 0.1 mile you'll pass the South Lost Lake Trail (which can be added to this hike—see Trail 14). Continue straight, eventually coming to a pretty waterfall in a sandstone bowl. Bear right at another road junction and reach the Lost Lake/Clayton Beach Trailhead at 2.2 miles. Then follow the Interurban Trail north 0.4 mile back to your start.

You can also follow the old Fragrance Lake Road left 0.8 mile to Cleator Road (elev. 1360 feet). From there you can walk on the road right for 0.9 mile to the Cyrus Gates Overlook (elev. 1850 feet) and return to Fragrance Lake via the steep 1 mile Double Black Diamond Trail. This trail is popular with mountain bikes—so be alert. At its steepest point the trail splits into two separate biker and hiker sections. The trail reaches the South Lost Lake Trail 0.1 mile from the Fragrance Lake Road junction.

Waterfall along Fragrance Lake Road

Fragrance Lake can also be reached from the Two Dollar Trail, which starts on Cleator Road about 0.6 mile from its junction with Chuckanut Drive (SR 11); parking is available. This lightly used trail traverses steep slopes, passing a beautiful waterfall and reaching Fragrance Lake at its outlet in 1.7 miles.

14 | Lost Lake

DISTANCE:	4.4 miles/9.6 miles/or 8.8 miles roundtrip
ELEVATION GAIN:	900 feet/1850 feet/2000 feet
HIGH POINT:	1625 feet/1400 feet/1300 feet
DIFFICULTY:	Moderate to difficult
FITNESS:	Hikers, runners
FAMILY-FRIENDLY:	No. Rock Trail contains steep steps—not suitable for young children. The other routes are too long for young children.
DOG-FRIENDLY:	On leash
AMENITIES:	Picnic tables, privy
CONTACT/MAP:	Larrabee State Park, Washington State Parks, Square One Maps: Chuckanut Recreation Area
GPS:	N 48° 39.212" W 122° 27.915"
BEFORE YOU GO:	A Discover Pass is required to park at the Rock Trail and Lost Lake Trail trailheads.

GETTING THERE

Driving to Rock Trail:

From Bellingham, follow I-5 south to Fairhaven exit 250. Head 0.1 mile west on Old Fairhaven Parkway and turn left onto 30th Street. Continue for 1 mile (the road becomes 32nd Street), turning right onto Old Samish Road. Then proceed for 0.6 mile, bearing left onto Chuckanut Drive (State Route 11). Continue 2.7 miles, turning left onto Hiline Road. Follow this road, which soon becomes Cleator Road (graveled), 3.6 miles to its end and the trailhead (elev. 1850 feet).

From Mount Vernon, head north on I-5 to exit 231. Follow SR 11 (Chuckanut Drive) north for 15.8 miles, turning right onto Hiline Road. Then follow this road, which soon becomes Cleator Road (graveled), 3.6 miles to its end.

Driving to Lost Lake Trail North:

From Bellingham, follow I-5 south to Fairhaven exit 250. Head 0.1 mile west on Old Fairhaven Parkway and turn left onto 30th

Street. Continue for 1 mile (the road becomes 32nd Street), turning right onto Old Samish Road. Then proceed for 0.6 mile, bearing left onto Chuckanut Drive (SR 11). Reach North Chuckanut Mountain Trailhead (elev. 60 feet) in 0.1 mile.

From Mount Vernon, follow I-5 north to exit 246 and drive west on Old Samish Road for 4.6 miles, bearing left onto Chuckanut Drive (SR 11); the trailhead is 0.1 mile farther.

Driving to Lost Lake Trail South:
From Bellingham, follow I-5 south to Fairhaven exit 250. Head 0.1 mile west on Old Fairhaven Parkway and turn left onto 30th Street. Continue for one mile (the road becomes 32nd Street) turning right onto Old Samish Road. Then proceed for 0.6 mile, bearing left onto Chuckanut Drive (SR 11). Continue 4.4 miles south to the Lost Lake Trailhead (elev. 200 feet).

From Mount Vernon, head north on I-5 to exit 231. Then follow SR 11 (Chuckanut Drive) north for 14.2 miles to the trailhead.

A long slender lake tucked within a fold of ledges, Lost Lake can be easily found, thanks to a series of good trails. However, none of the routes to this hidden body of water are easily hiked. The shortest way is the most interesting—starting high and descending via a series of steps along, beneath, and around big cliffs and ledges. The two longer routes follow old woods roads, making for excellent running routes. And no matter which route you take, be sure you go all the way to the lake's outlet, where an impressive cascade fans across a ledge shaded in deep timber.

GET MOVING
ROCK TRAIL
One of the more interesting and exciting trails in Larabee State Park, this fairly new trail was built by volunteers with the Washington Trails Association. From the lofty trailhead

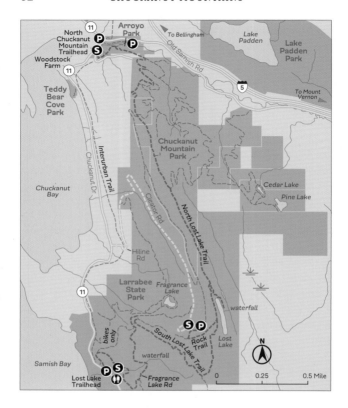

(which once provided sweeping views, now grown in), follow the Rock Trail west under a canopy of stately trees. At 0.2 mile come to a junction. The trail left leads 0.2 mile back to the parking lot, going over the Chuckanut Ridge highpoint. The trail right, called Double Black Diamond (and unofficially known as Chin Scraper), descends steeply to meet the Fragrance Lake Road Trail in 0.7 mile.

Continue straight, soon coming to quite an array of steps leading down off of the steep ridge. The trail descends rapidly. Enjoy peek-a-boo views of the Salish Sea and Blanchard

Lost Lake cradled in a fold of ledges

Mountain through the trees, but the real visual treats are the big sandstone ledges you are hiking beneath, along, and around. Marvel at the pockmarks, shallow caves, and honeycombs of the rock—a common sight in the outer San Juan Islands and Gulf Islands but quite rare on the Washington mainland.

The trail goes up and down along the ledges and winds around a few big boulders. Cross Bogaard's Bridge (named for the WTA crew leader) over a small creek and continue descending. At 1.2 miles, come to South Lost Lake Trail. Turn left and walk the sometimes muddy old road along the timbered ledge cradling Lost Lake below. You'll catch a few glimpses of the slender body of water before coming to a junction (elev. 1225 feet) at 1.8 miles.

The way left is the North Lost Lake Trail. Go right on the East Lost Lake Trail, soon coming to the muddy northern end of the lake. Hike a little farther along ledges, passing a few sunny spots before coming to Lost Lake's outlet at 2.2 miles. Here the outlet creek cascades over a steep ledge. It is easier to enjoy its music than to get a view of its show. Rest up for the return climb.

LOST LAKE TRAILHEAD

A long route to Lost Lake, primarily via old roads, this route makes for a nice run. Follow the Fragrance Lake Road on a gradual upward course, crossing a creek and coming to a junction at 1.1 miles. Continue left, soon returning to the creek crossed earlier. Here it cascades into a pretty little sandstone bowl—most impressive during the wet winter months. At 2.1 miles, reach a junction. Continuing straight ahead reaches Fragrance Lake. You want to go right, on the South Lost Lake Trail, beginning a long traverse of Chuckanut Ridge. Pass the Double Black Diamond Trail—a popular route with mountain bikers.

At 3.3 miles, crest a 1625-foot gap and begin a long, forested descent, reaching a junction with the Rock Trail at 3.8 miles. Continue right, reaching a junction with the North Lost Lake Trail at 4.4 miles. Then turn right, reaching Lost Lake's tumbling outlet creek at 4.8 miles.

NORTH CHUCKANUT MOUNTAIN TRAILHEAD

This long route to Lost Lake begins at this popular trailhead and primarily follows old roads, ideal for running. Follow the trail for 0.2 mile to the Interurban Trail. Then turn left and reach a junction at 0.5 mile. Head right, climbing through a beautiful grove of old-growth trees reaching a junction at 1 mile. Turn right here, reaching the Hemlock Trail at 1.2 miles. Then turn left on this old service road, coming to a junction at 1.4 miles. Head right on the North Lost Lake Trail—an old road—and follow it, passing many side trails (marked with good signs). The way gradually ascends to about 1300 feet before descending a little to Lost Lake.

At 4 miles, come to a junction (elev. 1225 feet) with the South Lost Lake Trail. Bear left, reaching the lake's outlet and a pretty cascade at 4.4 miles.

15 Chuckanut Ridge

DISTANCE:	10.8 miles roundtrip
ELEVATION GAIN:	2000 feet
HIGH POINT:	1750 feet
DIFFICULTY:	Difficult
FITNESS:	Hikers
FAMILY-FRIENDLY:	Yes, but some trails are also open to mountain bikes and horses. Use caution at ledges along the ridge. Not safe for young children.
DOG-FRIENDLY:	On leash
AMENITIES:	Benches

CONTACT/MAP:　Whatcom County Parks and Recreation,
Washington State Parks, Whatcom County Parks,
Larrabee State Park, Square One Maps:
Chuckanut Recreation Area
GPS:　N 48° 42.088" W 122° 29.348"

GETTING THERE

Driving: From Bellingham, follow I-5 south to Fairhaven exit
250. Head 0.1 mile west on Old Fairhaven Parkway and turn
left onto 30th Street. Continue for 1 mile (the road becomes

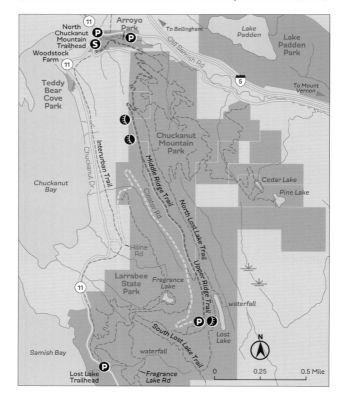

32nd Street), turning right onto Old Samish Road. Then proceed for 0.6 mile, bearing left onto Chuckanut Drive (State Route 11). Reach the trailhead in 0.1 mile.

From Mount Vernon, follow I-5 north to exit 246 and drive west on Old Samish Road for 4.6 miles, bearing left onto Chuckanut Drive; the trailhead is 0.1 mile farther.

A long rugged ridge of gnarled firs and sandstone ledges, Chuckanut Ridge offers challenging hiking and sweeping views. Follow the up-and-down ridge, clambering over steep knobs and stopping along the way to catch your breath and savor the scenery. Enjoy excellent views of Bellingham nestled below against a northern backdrop of icy BC peaks. And be wooed by the giant snow cone Mount Baker, hovering on the eastern horizon.

GET MOVING

From the busy North Chuckanut Mountain Trailhead (elev. 60 feet), follow the trail 0.2 mile to the Interurban Trail. Then turn left, cross a cascading creek, and reach a junction at 0.5 mile. Head right, climbing through a beautiful grove of old-growth trees, reaching a junction at 1 mile. Now turn right and climb some more, reaching the Hemlock Trail, an old service road, at 1.2 miles. Follow this trail 0.2 mile to a junction.

Turn right here and continue on the North Lost Lake Trail. Pass the Salal Trail and come to another junction (elev. 1100 feet) at 2.4 miles. Going straight takes you to Lost Lake (Trail 14); you want to go right on the Ridge Trail (which has Lower, Middle, and Upper named sections).

Now the fun begins. Wind beneath ledges and around boulders and then begin steeply climbing up Chuckanut Ridge. The way is rough, with copious rocks and roots to negotiate.

At 2.7 miles, reach the first (elev. 1350 feet) of several excellent viewpoints along this long ridge of sandstone cliffs

Mount Baker from Chuckanut Ridge

and ledges. Look north over Bellingham's Sehome Hill to BC's prominent Golden Ears and hundreds of other neighboring snowy summits. Look northeast at Sumas and Stewart mountains and to big, ever-impressive Mount Baker.

Now continue south through a small grove of pines followed by fir forest. The going is slow, with minor ups and downs. A few more viewpoints beg for you to take a break. Use caution at the viewpoints and keep dogs and children close by. The hum of I-5 fills the air but eventually fades as you continue along the ridge. At 3.2 miles, come to an unsigned junction (elev. 1350 feet) where the Lower Ridge Trail heads right, reaching Cleator Road (elev. 1250 feet) in 0.9 mile.

You want to continue left on a path now much rougher and brushier. Soon descend from a rocky knob, passing a wetland pool. Then continue dipping and climbing but slowly gaining net elevation. After topping a 1600-foot knoll, steeply descend about 100 feet on a rough and rocky route. Then climb again!

At 4.8 miles, come to another unmarked junction (elev. 1510 feet). Here a 0.2-mile path leads right to Cleator Road.

Your route is forward, soon coming to a good view of Mount Baker and Anderson Mountain. The trail continues to ascend, but at a much more agreeable grade, traversing thick stands of tenacious, wind-blasted firs. At 5.4 miles, the trail ends at a bend on Cleator Road (elev. 1750 feet). Here enjoy a window view of Mount Baker above Lake Samish. Then retrace your steps or consider the following options.

GO FARTHER

A trail leads left from the road bend, passing another viewpoint and heading over the 1870-foot ridge highpoint. In 0.4 mile it reaches a junction with the Rock Trail (see Trail 14), where you can walk right 0.2 to the Cyrus Gates Overlook (vegetation is obscuring the view) at the end of Cleator Road, then walk 0.25 mile down the road back to the Chuckanut Ridge Trail.

You can make an adventurous 12.2-mile loop by following the Rock Trail 1.2 miles to the Lost Lake Trail, then hiking north on that trail 2.8 miles back to the junction with the Ridge Trail. From there retrace your earlier steps 2.4 miles back to your start.

16 Clayton Beach

DISTANCE:	1.2 miles roundtrip
ELEVATION GAIN:	200 feet
HIGH POINT:	200 feet
DIFFICULTY:	Moderate
FITNESS:	Hikers
FAMILY-FRIENDLY:	Yes, but steep ledge and dangerous RR crossing
DOG-FRIENDLY:	On leash
AMENITIES:	Privy

CONTACT/MAP:	Washington State Parks, Larrabee State Park
	Square One Maps: Chuckanut Recreation Area
GPS:	N 48° 38.899" W 122° 29.252"
BEFORE YOU GO:	A Discover Pass is required

GETTING THERE

Driving: From Bellingham, follow I-5 south to Fairhaven exit 250. Head 0.1 mile west on Old Fairhaven Parkway and turn left onto 30th Street. Continue for 1 mile (the road becomes 32nd Street), turning right onto Old Samish Road. Then proceed for 0.6 mile, bearing left onto Chuckanut Drive (State Route 11). Continue 4.4 miles south to the Lost Lake Trailhead (elev. 200 feet).

From Mount Vernon, head north on I-5 to exit 231. Then follow SR 11 (Chuckanut Drive) north for 14.2 miles to the trailhead.

One of the most picturesque strands of sand on Samish Bay, Clayton Beach is popular with Western Washington University students, birders, sun worshippers, the occasional sea lion, and just about everyone else. On a warm sunny summer weekend, it can get downright crowded on this small stretch of beach. The trail is a bit rough but well trod. Plan your visit on a low tide and wander a third of a mile of beautiful tidal flats.

GET MOVING

From near the parking lot entrance, carefully cross Chuckanut Drive (SR 11) and locate the trailhead. Descend a staircase and come to a junction. This is part of the old 27-mile-long Bellingham and Skagit Interurban Railway, which operated from 1912 to 1930. The stretch from Clayton Beach to Bellingham's Fairhaven District has been converted to trail. However, this short section south to the beach is much rougher than the northern 6.6 miles of trail. Washington State Parks will eventually upgrade it—and a long-needed pedestrian bridge over the active rail line should be in place sometime in 2017.

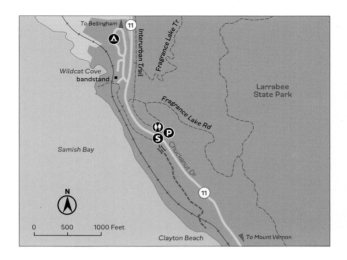

Now turn left and start descending, immediately crossing a cascading creek on a steel bridge. The way cuts through a thick jungle-like forest and sandstone ledges. Eventually, the trail will be far enough below and away from the parallel SR 11 that you no longer hear cars and motorcycles puttering by.

At 0.5 mile the trail departs from the old rail bed, heading right down a steep section of ledge that may give some folks a few—albeit not major—problems. Hopefully, however, by the time of your visit the new pedestrian bridge over the adjacent active railroad tracks (thanks to a grant by the Washington Wildlife and Recreation Coalition) will be in place, eliminating this steep section and dangerous crossing. In the meantime, use extreme caution crossing the tracks—look both ways and scamper quickly. And do not under any circumstances walk along or on these tracks (it's trespassing and extremely dangerous).

Once you wind up on the right side of the tracks, continue on a single track, dropping down to beautiful Clayton Beach with its sandy coves tucked between sandstone ledges and

Sea lion sunning at Clayton Beach

a short, wide strand of sandy beach. You can walk a short way north and south, watching for marine birds and mammals and enjoying serene Salish Sea scenery. Directly across Samish Bay are Samish, Guemes, Vendovi, Cypress, and Lummi islands.

At the south end, locate some old trestle piles. These are the remains of a 4-mile section of the old Interurban Rail that went right above the water here—giving the line the nickname of the "trolley that went to sea." It must have been one heck of a ride—as this is one beautiful hike.

GO FARTHER

Hike back to the staircase, and instead of returning to the parking lot, continue straight on a delightful path through madronas and along ledges granting decent views across the water. This trail leads 0.3 mile to the main day-use area of Larrabee State Park. From here you can hike a short path to a beach on Wildcat Cove or take the Fragrance Lake Trail to the Interurban Trail and hike back to your vehicle.

17 Squires Lake

DISTANCE:	2 miles of trails
ELEVATION GAIN:	Up to 400 feet
HIGH POINT:	650 feet
DIFFICULTY:	Easy to moderate
FITNESS:	Walkers, hikers, runners
FAMILY-FRIENDLY:	Yes, but trails also open to bikes and horses; use caution on the South Ridge Trail
DOG-FRIENDLY:	On leash
AMENITIES:	Privy, benches
CONTACT/MAP:	Whatcom County Parks and Recreation, Skagit Parks and Recreation, Square One Maps: Chuckanut Recreation Area
GPS:	N 48° 38. 620" W 122° 21.320"

GETTING THERE

Driving: From Bellingham, follow I-5 south to Lake Samish exit 242. From Mount Vernon, follow I-5 north to exit 242. Then drive southeast on Old Highway 99 for 0.7 mile to the park trailhead and parking on your left.

A former family fish and fur farm, Squires Lake is now a wonderful little 82-acre park. Straddling the Whatcom–Skagit county line, Squires Lake is cooperatively managed by both counties' parks departments. A family favorite for folks from both Bellingham and Mount Vernon, located just off of busy I-5, Squires Lake also offers walkers, hikers, and trail runners in transit a quick nature fix.

GET MOVING

From the trailhead, follow a well-used, well-graded trail beneath a canopy of big maples. The way utilizes a portion of an old logging railroad bed. You'll immediately get your heart

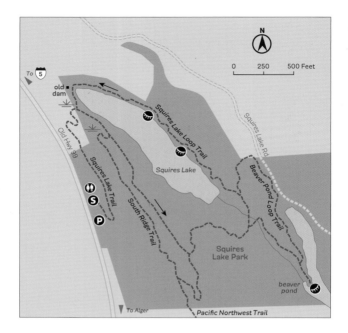

rate up, climbing 140 feet in 0.3 mile, coming to a junction at Squires Lake.

Here, take the popular 0.9-mile loop around the lake. Mainly via a wide, old woods road, this trail travels through mature second-growth forest on gently rolling terrain above the lake's southern shoreline. The trail then descends to cross the lake's inlet stream before hugging its northern shoreline. Pass a couple of lovely viewpoints complete with benches, ideal for taking a break and scanning the lake for waterfowl. The way crosses some marshy wetlands on a boardwalk before running alongside the lake to the small, old dam that was built to create this body of water.

Close the loop and return to the trailhead for a 1.5-mile workout. If you're looking for more, consider these options.

A rare winter freeze at Squires Lake

The 0.5-mile South Ridge Trail loop adds about 0.2 mile to the lake loop if used as an alternate route. This trail takes off east not far from the main junction and climbs 200 feet along the ridge. There's a good viewpoint over the Friday Creek Valley to Blanchard Mountain.

PACIFIC NORTHWEST TRAIL

During the backpacking boom of the 1970s, transplanted New Englander Ron Strickland was struck with a novel idea. How about adding another classic long-distance hiking trail to our country's stock? One to accompany and rival the likes of the Appalachian, Pacific Crest, and Colorado Divide Trails. So began his quest to build the Pacific Northwest Trail (PNT), a 1200-mile path from Cape Alava on the Olympic Peninsula to Montana's Glacier National Park.

Soon forming the Pacific Northwest Trail Association, Strickland and a slew of tireless volunteers set out promoting, constructing, and maintaining the new trail. Utilizing existing trails along with new tread, the PNT travels across Fidalgo Island and the Chuckanut Mountains on its way from the Pacific to the Rockies. While parts of the trail still follow roads, much progress is being made on completing the PNT since 2009, when President Obama signed a bill designating it a national scenic trail—a status shared by the Pacific Crest Trail (PCT) and Appalachian Trail (AT).

You can hike or run along portions of the PNT on the following trails in this book: Squires Lake (Trail 17), Oyster Dome (Trail 18), Lizard and Lily lakes (Trail 19), Padilla Bay Dike Trail (Trail 28), Tommy Thompson Trail (Trail 36), Anacortes Community Forest Lands (Trails 40 and 41), and Deception Pass State Park (Trail 43). Visit www.pnt.org for more information.

The Pacific Northwest Trail (see sidebar) veers right off of the South Ridge Trail, leaving the park. It continues via an easement, climbing the ridge through private timberlands. There are a couple of decent viewpoints along the way, but they include steep drops, making this section of trail not recommended for young children.

On the main lake loop near the lake's inlet stream, the lovely Beaver Pond Loop leaves for a 0.5 mile journey to—big surprise here—a beaver pond before returning to the main loop. The trail crosses the cascading inlet creek and climbs

75 feet through a forest of big, old cedar stumps showing springboard notches. Loggers of yesteryear used crosscut saws to fell these once humongous trees by standing on boards notched into the trunks just above their fluted bases. This is a great trail for kids, with its logging history and wildlife watching opportunities.

GO FARTHER

A few miles south on Old Highway 99 (just north of the Bow Hill Road junction), find the Pomona Grange Park, a delightful little Skagit County Park little known by most area residents. Here explore two short interpretive trails.

18 Oyster Dome

DISTANCE:	6.2 miles roundtrip
ELEVATION GAIN:	1900 feet
HIGH POINT:	2025 feet
DIFFICULTY:	Strenuous
FITNESS:	Hikers, runners
FAMILY-FRIENDLY:	Yes, but use caution on summit ledges
DOG-FRIENDLY:	On leash
CONTACT/MAP:	Washington State Department of Natural Resources Northwest Region Office (Sedro-Woolley) Square One Maps: Chuckanut Recreation Area
GPS:	N 48° 36.522' W 122° 26.000'
BEFORE YOU GO:	A Discover Pass is required to park at the eastside trailhead.

GETTING THERE

Driving: From Mount Vernon, head north on I-5 to exit 231. Follow State Route 11 (Chuckanut Drive) north for 10.2 miles. The trailhead (elev. 150 feet) is located on the right side of the road just after passing Milepost 10. Limited parking is on the left (west) shoulder of the highway. Be sure to park well out of traveled road lanes and away from posted areas (or risk being towed).

From Bellingham, follow SR 11 south for 11.2 miles to the trailhead. An alternative approach with plenty of parking is via the eastern trailhead (see Trail 19 for directions).

A glacially polished and fractured exposed hunk of sheer cliff on Blanchard Mountain, the Oyster Dome is an intriguing and scenic natural landmark. Here, where the Cascades meet the Salish Sea, the Oyster Dome looms 2000 feet above salty waters. The dome's base is littered with jumbled boulders, talus heaps, and bat-breeding caves. And from atop, views abound of sound, strait, mountains, and a smorgasbord of islands. A popular hiking destination year-round, the Oyster Dome is the pearl of the Chuckanut Mountains.

GET MOVING

Your route begins on the Chuckanut Trail, which also happens to be part of the Pacific Northwest Trail, a 1200-mile route from the Olympic Coast to Montana's Glacier National Park (see sidebar). Follow the well-built and well-trod path through a mostly uniform forest of second-growth conifers. A few big Douglas firs here and there break the canopy monotony. The way climbs steadily, but a few sweeping switchbacks ease the pain.

At just over a mile, reach a bench at a small ledge with big views out to the San Juan Islands and Olympic Mountains—a teaser of what lies ahead. At 1.5 miles, reach a junction (elev. 1075 feet). This junction, like most throughout the Blanchard State Forest, has recently been graced with big, bold new signs. Now head left on the Samish Bay Trail, traversing Blanchard's western slopes and skirting a recent cut and hopping across a few small creeks in the process.

Stunning Salish Sea and San Juan Islands view from the Oyster Dome

Pass an unmarked trail leading left to private property. The way now steepens, entering a damp, dark glen littered with big boulders and cradling a small tributary of Oyster Creek. This section of trail used to be a rough-and-tumble mess, but it has been greatly improved—complete with switchbacks—thanks to the Washington Trail Association's volunteer crews. Steadily climb, passing giant erratics, old springboard-notched cedar stumps, and an ice age interpretive sign.

At 2.8 miles, reach another junction (elev. 1875 feet). Now head left on the Oyster Dome Trail, passing rusty cables and other old logging relics. Slightly descend to cross a small creek, then make one final push on a steep, rooty trail. At 3.1 miles, break out of the forest onto the rocky rim of Oyster Dome. Be careful. Keep children and dogs nearby. Oyster Dome's abrupt drop of more than 400 feet may lead you to clam

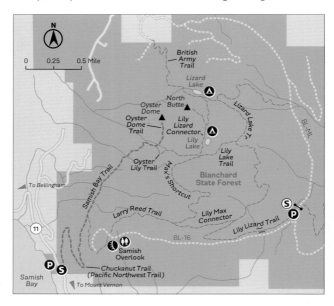

up. Its views, however, are succulent. Spread out before you are the San Juan Islands; Fidalgo, Whidbey, and Vancouver islands; the snow-capped Olympic Mountains; a patchwork of farms in the Skagit River Flats; and a whole lot of saltwater. Count islands, watch boats, and, if it's a fair day, soak up the sun's rays.

While savoring this stunning scenery, note that much of this recreational and biological gem between Bellingham and Mount Vernon was once slated to be logged. But due to the work of Conservation Northwest and other local organizations, a consensus has been reached with the Department of Natural Resources to protect Blanchard's core, which includes Oyster Dome. However, if the legislature doesn't come up with funding in 2017 for a land purchase elsewhere to allow logging, the core of Blanchard may end up being harvested.

GO FARTHER

For an excellent loop that adds a little distance and a reprieve from the crowds, consider the following option. From the Oyster Dome Trail junction, continue east on the Oyster Lily Trail, following along a creek for 0.5 mile to a junction (elev. 2000 feet). Here you can go left and explore Lily Lake (Trail 19), or continue right a few more feet to another junction. Turn right here onto Max's Shortcut and enjoy a pleasant descent, reaching another junction at 1.9 miles. Continue right on the Larry Reed Trail, soon traversing a recent clear-cut. Then cross two logging roads and pass through an attractive forest grove before reaching the Samish Overlook (elev. 1300 feet) at 2.8 miles. Here find a popular spot (complete with privy) for hang glider launching—and breathtaking views south over Samish Bay and the Skagit Flats. Then pick up the Chuckanut Trail and descend, coming to the familiar Samish Bay Trail junction at 3.2 miles. Head left and downhill and once again encounter a lot of fellow trail users, reaching your start at 4.7 miles.

19   Lizard and Lily Lakes

DISTANCE:	7.5 miles roundtrip
ELEVATION GAIN:	1500 feet
HIGH POINT:	2100 feet
DIFFICULTY:	Moderate
FITNESS:	Hikers, runners
FAMILY-FRIENDLY:	Yes, but trails also open to bikes and horses
DOG-FRIENDLY:	On leash
AMENITIES:	Benches, backcountry campsites, privy
CONTACT/MAP:	Washington State Department of Natural Resources; Northwest Region Office (Sedro-Woolley) Square One Maps: Chuckanut Recreation Area
GPS:	N 48° 36.933" W 122° 23.230"
BEFORE YOU GO:	A Discover Pass is required to park at the trailheads.

GETTING THERE

Driving: From Mount Vernon, drive north 14 miles on I-5 to Alger exit 240; from Bellingham, follow I-5 south 12 miles to Alger exit 240. Turn left (northwest) onto Lake Samish Road and drive 0.5 mile. Then turn left onto Barrel Springs Road and proceed for 0.7 mile. Turn right onto DNR Road BL-ML (unpaved) and continue for 1.7 miles (passing Lower Trailhead, with privy) to a junction. Left goes to the Samish Overlook; go right 0.2 mile to Upper Trailhead parking.

Two little backcountry lakes on the back side of the Oyster Dome, Lizard and Lily, offer much easier and quieter rambling than the Blanchard State Forest's more famous feature. The east side of Blanchard, with its gated logging roads and inter-connecting trails, offers more loop options too. You can easily spend all day—or even overnight here, with several backcoun-try campsites. Trail runners can get quite a workout here with both long-distance options and decent elevation gain. And

North Butte offers some fine views for those willing to go the extra distance on this loop.

GET MOVING

The way described here is a loop and makes for an excellent moderate all-day hike or decent trail run. From the Upper Trailhead (elev. 875 feet), walk 0.1 mile back down the road you drove up, coming to the Lily Lizard Trail. Here a kiosk shows the trail system of the Blanchard State Forest. This trailhead, like all of the junctions along the way, is well marked with attractive, durable signage.

The way parallels a forest road (BL-16) west for a short way, contouring along south-facing slopes. Cross a cascading creek on a good bridge and continue easy walking. Parts of the trail follow an old logging railroad—look for rails. Next, the way switchbacks east, coming to a junction

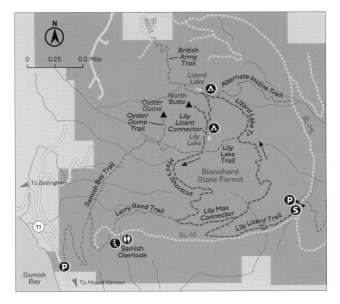

(elev. 1375 feet) with the Lily Max Connector at 1.4 miles. You'll be returning left, so continue right.

Soon you'll come to a familiar cascading creek, here crossed sans bridge. The way then climbs more steadily, going up and over and around a few bumps on the ridge before coming to a junction (elev. 2000 feet) with the Lily Lake Trail at 2.6 miles. That trail takes off left, reaching Lily Lake in 0.7 mile. The loop now continues right on the Lizard Lake Trail, part of the long-distance Pacific Northwest Trail (see sidebar).

Utilizing an old logging railroad bed, the way traverses steep slopes adorned with big stumps a century old and shrouded in mature second growth. At 3.1 miles, come to another junction (elev. 1900 feet). Here the Alternate Incline Trail heads right, steeply descending to reach a gated BL-ML road in 1.1 miles. From there it is a 1-mile trek right to the Upper Trailhead.

You want to continue left, coming to a junction at Lizard Lake (elev. 1860 feet) in 3.4 miles. Here a short spur leads right to a camping area on the shallow lake's southeast shore. Take a break here and enjoy the serenity, then return to the junction. The lightly hiked British Army Trail, straight ahead, descends 1.2 miles to the BL-4803 road. From there it's 0.2 mile to the BL-ML road, which can then be followed 3 miles right to the Upper Trailhead.

The loop continues left on the Lizard Lily Connector Trail. Follow this rougher trail upward, passing a massive glacial erratic and a few big trees as well. At 3.7 miles, reach a junction (elev. 2100 feet) at a saddle. The trail right is a rough but well worthwhile side trip. This trail travels 0.2 mile to ledges (use caution) on 2200-foot North Butte, with excellent views east to Mount Baker; and to the northwest of Vendovi, Sinclair, Orcas, Lummi, Clark, and Barnes islands as well as BC's Saturna and Vancouver islands.

From the junction, the trail slowly descends, soon coming to Lily Lake (elev. 2000 feet) with its backcountry campsites. This little lake is a good spot to watch for waterfowl and

Appropriately named Lily Lake

beavers. The trail continues south along a stream dammed by beavers and reaches a junction at 4 miles. The trail right goes to the Oyster Dome (Trail 18). You want to go left, immediately coming to a junction.

Now head right on Max's Shortcut Trail (also part of the PNT), traversing a thickly forested ridge. Then slowly descend, crossing a small creek in a dark hollow. The way then steadily loses elevation, reaching a junction (elev. 1450 feet) with the Larry Reed and Lily Max Connector trails at 5.4 miles. The trail right goes to the Samish Overlook (Trail 18). Go left on a fairly level trail contouring along south-facing slopes. At 6.1 miles, return to a familiar junction. Head right and return to the Upper Trailhead at 7.5 miles.

GO FARTHER

You can extend your hike or run with trips to the nearby Oyster Dome. You can also make a much longer loop by following the gated BL-ML road and British Army Trails (as already described).

Next page: *Old logging railroad trestles in Lake Whatcom*

WESTERN WHATCOM COUNTY

Consisting of Salish Sea shoreline, flat and fertile farmlands, and forested Cascade foothills, Bellingham's hinterlands are quite pastoral and picturesque. Perpetually snow-covered Mount Baker looming in the distance can be seen from just about every corner of the county's western reaches. Interspersed with fields of raspberries, blueberries, strawberries, hay, horses, and cows, are a handful of quaint communities—among them Ferndale, Blaine, and Lynden. Here you'll find fine parks and preserves with wonderful trails— climbing forested mountains, meandering across historic farms and homesteads, and reaching and skirting dramatic beaches and bays.

20 Stimpson Family Nature Reserve

DISTANCE:	4 miles of trails
ELEVATION GAIN:	Up to 350 feet
HIGH POINT:	825 feet
DIFFICULTY:	Easy to moderate
FITNESS:	Hikers
FAMILY-FRIENDLY:	Yes
DOG-FRIENDLY:	Dogs prohibited
AMENITIES:	Benches, privy
CONTACT/MAP:	Whatcom County Parks and Recreation
GPS:	N 48° 43.958" W 122° 22.679"

GETTING THERE

Driving: From Bellingham, follow I-5 to exit 253. Then follow Lakeway Drive east for 2.7 miles onto Terrace Avenue. Continue 0.2 mile onto Cable Street. After 0.3 mile, turn right onto Austin Street. Proceed for 0.4 mile, bearing left onto Lake Louise Road. Then drive 1.1 miles to the trailhead located on your left.

Transit: Whatcom Transit Route 512 to Sudden Valley

The Stimpson Family Nature Reserve encompasses more than 350 acres of mature forest and two wildlife-rich wetlands on a ridge above Lake Whatcom. Whatcom County Parks manages this natural tract between Bellingham and Sudden Valley. But it came to be via various conservation-minded folks. The reserve began in 2001 through an initial land donation from the Stimpson Family to the Whatcom Land Trust. Subsequent land donations from Western Washington University were soon added, along with the adjoining Washington State Department of Natural Resources' Lake Louise Natural Resources Conservation Area. All of the groups agreed for this special place to be a reserve and not a

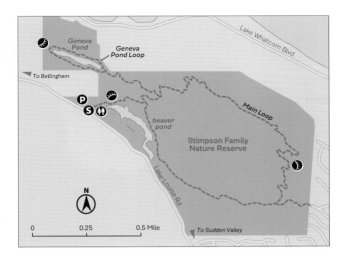

park—a place for quiet reflection and an outdoor classroom for introducing children to nature. No bikes, dogs, or horses are allowed. Walk these trails with all of your senses attuned to the natural world around you—and return through the seasons for new perspectives.

GET MOVING

The four miles of trail within the reserve are a real treat to hike, thanks to Russ Pfeiffer-Hoyt, a master trail builder with the Whatcom Land Trust. "When Russ builds a trail, it is not simply a way to get you from one place to another," says the trust. You'll quickly agree as you wander through groves of towering trees, dart through and around dark ravines, and meander alongside placid pools of water.

From the trailhead, immediately enter a grove of big trees, cross a creek, and skirt a large beaver pond. Then come to a good viewpoint of the large wetland. Look for sights and signs of the industrious rodents as well as a myriad of birds. In 0.3 mile,

Geneva Pond

reach a junction and the start of the main loop. Go left or right on this 2.6-mile loop. If you go left, you'll drop into a small ravine—cross a creek on another attractive bridge and within 0.1 mile reach another junction. Here the 1.2-mile Geneva Pond loop heads to the left.

This wonderful loop is fine on its own—especially for young children—or makes a great add-on to the main loop, for a much longer outing and bigger calorie burner. Take this trail left through more big, old trees—some more than 400 years old—and alongside a wetland. Cross a creek and reach a junction at 0.3 mile. Here the trail loops 0.6 mile around Geneva Pond. You'll pass an old dam where you get excellent views of the pond, which often reflects the towering timber lining its shoreline. A granite bench here allows for sitting and gazing out at the water. Birding here is excellent. Once you circle the pond, retrace your steps 0.3 mile back to the Main Loop.

The Main Loop continues east, skirting more wetlands and traversing more impressive forest. Pass two giant Douglas firs and climb. The trail weaves and switchbacks up and along folds in the ridge. Pass another granite bench near the trail's high point. Then descend, passing a spur that leads left 0.2 mile to Sudden Valley.

The way then follows an old skid road as you again approach the big beaver pond. Reenter old forest and look for younger trees that have succumbed to the resident beavers' master plan for the area. Then return to the first junction, where it's 0.3 mile to the left back to the trailhead. If you hiked only the Geneva Pond Loop, record 2 miles in your fitness log. Did the Main Loop? Write down 3.2 miles. Knocked out both loops? That's 4.4 miles.

21 Lookout Mountain Forest Preserve

DISTANCE:	More than 4 miles of trails
ELEVATION GAIN:	Up to 850 feet
HIGH POINT:	1300 feet
DIFFICULTY:	Easy to moderate
FITNESS:	Hikers, runners
FAMILY-FRIENDLY:	Yes
DOG-FRIENDLY:	On leash
AMENITIES:	Privy, benches
CONTACT/MAP:	Whatcom County Parks and Recreation
GPS:	N 48° 43.134" W 122° 21.316"

GETTING THERE

Driving: From Bellingham, follow I-5 to exit 253. Then follow Lakeway Drive east for 2.7 miles onto Terrace Avenue. Continue 0.2 mile onto Cable Street. After 0.3 mile, turn right onto Austin Street. Proceed for 0.4 mile, bearing left onto Lake Louise Road. Then drive 2.5 miles to the trailhead on the right across from Sudden Valley Gate no. 9.

Transit: Whatcom Transit Route 512 to Sudden Valley

The Lookout Mountain Forest Preserve consists of the northern portion of the new Lookout Mountain Park. Created in 2014 through private timberland acquisition and land reconveyed from the Department of Natural Resources, 4430-acre Lookout Mountain Park will eventually host a large interconnecting trail system. But for now, you can enjoy hiking and

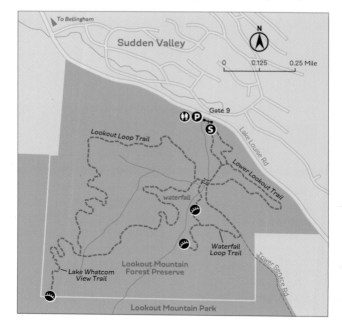

running on more than 4 miles of well-built and signed trails within the preserve—and miles of old service roads outside of the preserve. Just don't expect much of a lookout from Lookout, as the forest canopy here is pretty thick, making this a good choice on an overcast day.

GET MOVING

While popular with Sudden Valley residents taking their pups out for a walk, the Lookout Mountain Forest Preserve is still off the radar for many area residents. That probably won't hold true for long once Whatcom County Parks begins working on a major trail expansion here. Until then, enjoy fairly peaceful ambling on the preserve's current trail network.

From the trailhead, choose whether to hike the Lower Lookout Trail or head up the gated unpaved service road to the Lookout Loop and Waterfall Loop trails. Of course, you can combine them all for a good figure-eight hike of 5 miles. Here's what you can expect:

LOWER LOOKOUT TRAIL

This trail immediately leaves the trailhead and makes a couple of short switchbacks before making a long sweep to the service road. It travels mostly through dank, younger forest and passes a few small wetland pools. The trail is 0.75 mile and gains less than 100 feet. From here you can turn right and return to the trailhead in 0.25 mile via the service road or cross the road and continue hiking on the Waterfall Loop and/or Lookout Loop trails.

WATERFALL LOOP TRAIL

Reach this trail by hiking or running 0.25 mile up the gated service road to a trail junction. Turn right and immediately turn left at a second junction. Then climb about 100 feet in 0.15 mile to an overlook on a steep ravine edge—keep the kids nearby. Peer through mossy trees to a cascade fanning down

Stately and uniform second-growth forest on Lookout Mountain

the slickrock. It's most impressive in the winter—and barely a trickle later in the year.

From here the loop continues, reaching a junction at 0.2 mile after another 50 feet of climbing. You can hike right 0.2 mile, climbing another 50 feet to a spot on the creek, passing two large parallel nurse logs. Or you can head left, descending and reaching the service road in 0.2 mile. From here it's 0.4 mile to the left back to the trailhead.

LOOKOUT LOOP TRAIL

This is a nice little loop with a good climb of 850 feet, giving you a decent workout. To reach this trail, hike or run 0.25 mile up the gated service road to a trail junction. Then turn right and immediately come to another junction. Stay right, cross a small creek, and soon come to a junction with the Lookout Loop. The way right is steeper, so head that way, saving your knees for an easier descent.

The way follows old logging roads and newly built trail, passing some big maples among stands of alders and young conifers. At about 0.5 mile the way steepens, passing some big cedars en route. After some tight switchbacks the trail passes through a gap and reaches a junction (elev. 950 feet) at 1.2 miles.

Here the Lake Whatcom View Trail takes off to the right. Hike for the workout, not the lookout! This trail climbs steeply—350 feet—to a bench at a growing-in window view of Mount Baker and Lake Whatcom in 0.4 mile. Prior to reaching the disappointing viewpoint, the trail passes a row of cedars and another window view—this one of Stewart Mountain. Heart rate now up, retrace your steps back to the junction.

Then continue on the Lookout Loop Trail, following an old logging road and descending. Pass a viewpoint of a small slickrock cascade before closing the loop in 0.9 mile. Turn right and hike 0.1 mile back to the service road. The total mileage of the loop with the Lake Lookout spur from the trailhead is 3.6 miles.

GO FARTHER

If you're up for a good workout and don't mind miles of trees and no views, consider hiking or running to one or both of Lookout Mountain's communications tower–topped summits. Continue up the graveled service road, skirting a Sudden Valley neighborhood before entering thick, mature second growth. The forest is open and actually quite attractive, with

RECONVEYANCE TO RECREATION

Bellingham is already one of the Northwest's premier trail towns—and it's about to get a whole lot better. In March of 2013, after much commentary from citizens, conservationists, and recreationists, and at the urging of both the Whatcom Land Trust and Conservation Northwest, the Whatcom County Council voted five to two to reconvey 8844 acres of state DNR land bordering Lake Whatcom to the county. What does this mean? Better protection for Bellingham's water supply, for one thing. And a whole heck of a lot more land for recreation since the transferred lands will be managed primarily as parkland. And at nearly 9000 acres, this new Whatcom Lake Park qualifies as one of the largest urban parks in America.

Much of the reconveyed land had previously been used for timber production and now will be managed primarily for nonmotorized recreation: hiking, mountain biking, and horseback riding. Whatcom County Parks and Recreation has plans to construct about 55 miles of trails on the two parcels making up the new park. Separated by the lake, the eastern tract on Mount Stewart and the western tract on Lookout Mountain both contain a series of logging and communications tower service roads.

The parcel on Mount Stewart was more intensively logged and is bisected by a wide powerline right of way, but it still offers both large stands of mature timber and breathtaking views. The Lookout Mountain parcel comprises older timber and has a wilder and more natural feel. The Lookout Mountain section also currently has a network of well-built trails, while the Stewart Mountain section is traversed by miles of mostly poorly built user trails, some of which will eventually be upgraded and/or decommissioned.

The trail system will move forward as funding is secured. And a large contingent of local volunteer trail-building groups are ready to chip in—ensuring that new trails should be cropping up here soon. The addition of such a large park to the impressive county and city park system further enhances the quality of life in Bellingham, already an uncontested trail and fitness hub in the Northwest.

many creeks you'll cross along the way. Most of the elevation gain is gradual, but there are a couple of steep spots and one long dip giving up some elevation. At 3.6 miles from the trailhead, reach a Y-junction (elev. 2000 feet). Head left 1.4 miles for the lower (not by much) 2676-foot summit. Here you'll find communications towers, but no view.

Head right 1.5 miles for the taller (not by much) 2677-foot summit. Here find communications towers and a tiny view of Mount Baker east and the Skagit Flats, Salish Sea, and a handful of islands to the west. Absolutely do not trespass within the gated tower complexes and restricted road below the summit. Years ago there were fire lookouts on these summits—and views—but that's all in the past. Enjoy the long trip out.

22 Lake Whatcom Park: Hertz Trail

DISTANCE:	6.2 miles roundtrip
ELEVATION GAIN:	60 feet
HIGH POINT:	375 feet
DIFFICULTY:	Easy
FITNESS:	Hikers, walkers, and runners
FAMILY-FRIENDLY:	Yes, wide, level trail; the first 2 miles are easy for pushing a jogging stroller
DOG-FRIENDLY:	On leash
AMENITIES:	Benches, historical kiosks, privies
CONTACT/MAP:	Whatcom County Parks and Recreation
GPS:	N 48° 43.817" W 122° 18.497"

GETTING THERE

Driving: From Bellingham, follow I-5 to exit 253. Then follow Lakeway Drive east for 1.7 miles, bearing left onto Electric Avenue. Continue 1.1 miles, bearing right onto Northshore Drive, which becomes Northshore Road. Follow Northshore Road for 7.2 miles, bearing left at the road split. Then continue for 0.5 mile to the trailhead (elev. 375 feet) on your left. The

First of two covered bridges along Hertz Trail

wheelchair-accessible trailhead is 0.2 mile farther on North-shore Road.

Follow an old logging railroad bed along the quiet and fairly wild northern shore of massive Lake Whatcom, one of the largest natural lakes in the state. The shores of this lake once bustled with townships, mills, and mines. Now homes dot much of its southern shore; here, along the lake's northeastern shore, parkland graces this important body of water. The Hertz Trail, named for a former mayor and city parks director, utilizes a nearly level rail bank, hugging the forested shore of this glacial-trough lake. Enjoy waterfalls and quiet beaches along the way as well as old-growth forest groves, shoreline ledges, and a couple of covered bridges.

GET MOVING

From the large parking area, two trails of equal distance take off for Lake Whatcom through a dark, cool cedar grove. At 0.2 mile, after a descent of about 60 feet, reach the old rail bed. The way right leads 0.2 mile west to the wheelchair access trailhead and small parking lot. Go left immediately, coming to an arch made from a part of an original trestle once serving

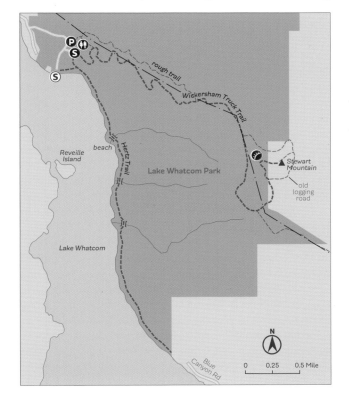

this old rail line. Take some time to read all of the interpretive panels and try to imagine what this lake—now Bellingham's water supply—looked like a century ago when it bustled with boats and logs and mining operations.

Now prepare for a tranquil (especially in winter, when boats are absent) hike or run along an undeveloped lakeshore. In 2015 much of the high slopes abutting the lake along this trail corridor became a Whatcom County Park. Part of 8844 acres reconveyed from the Washington DNR to the county, these lands now form one of the largest urban parks in the state. County officials are exploring the possibility of developing more than 50 miles of new trails here and at the Lookout Mountain parcel.

Pass numerous small beaches popular with pooches and people on warm summer days. The trail is marked with distance posts every half mile. At 1 mile, come to a little cascade and a covered bridge spanning the tumbling creek just downstream. Here, too, find one of the prettiest beaches along the trail, complete with a bench and good views of Reveille Island directly across the lake. This is a good turning-around spot for a short outing. Otherwise continue, soon coming to a section of trail traversing ledges directly alongside the lake. Keep dogs and children nearby to prevent an unexpected plunge.

Pass beneath sandstone ledges and a remaining section of old trestle. Pass, too, remnant pockets of old-growth forest. Rare marbled murrelets nest in some of these ancient groves. Soon after passing through another covered bridge, come to a particularly large Douglas fir. The wide, well-groomed trail then gets a little rougher but is still generally an easy hike. Pass through maple glades, fir groves, and hillsides sporting madronas. At 3.1 miles the trail ends. County officials hope to someday extend this trail to Blue Canyon Road at the lake's southeast corner. For now, however, retrace your steps; take a rest at one of the nicely placed benches and scan the water for loons, golden-eyes, dippers, and spotted sandpipers.

23 Lake Whatcom Park: Stewart Mountain

DISTANCE:	9 miles roundtrip
ELEVATION GAIN:	2550 feet
HIGH POINT:	2900 feet
DIFFICULTY:	Strenuous
FITNESS:	Hikers and runners
FAMILY-FRIENDLY:	No
DOG-FRIENDLY:	On leash
AMENITIES:	Privy
CONTACT/MAP:	Whatcom County Parks and Recreation
GPS:	N 48° 43.810" W 122° 18.439"

GETTING THERE

Driving: From Bellingham, follow I-5 to exit 253. Then follow Lakeway Drive east for 1.7 miles, bearing left onto Electric Avenue. Then continue 1.1 miles, bearing right onto Northshore Drive. Follow Northshore Drive, which becomes Northshore Road for 7.2 miles, bearing left at the road split. Then continue for 0.5 mile to the trailhead (elev. 350 feet) on your left.

It's a long, lung-busting, quad-burning way to this lofty knob on the Stewart Mountain massif. But the views—Mount Baker, the Twin Sisters, and massive fjord-like Lake Whatcom sparkling directly below—are what truly take your breath away. And more—the San Juan Islands, and BC's Gulf Islands. You'll be following a powerline swath, however, so this isn't the most aesthetically pleasing route. But it's lightly traveled and offers a great workout, and again, the views beyond the massive towers are simply divine.

GET MOVING

Recently added to Whatcom County's growing and exceptional park system through the Lake Whatcom Reconveyance

Enjoy a sweeping Lake Whatcom view from Stewart Mountain.

(see Reconveyance to Recreation sidebar), Stewart Mountain will eventually contain a top-notch trail system. But in the meantime you'll have to be content with hiking or running either a logging trunk road that's closed to vehicles, or a very steep and unmarked user-built trail. The road is the preferred route, being easier to follow and sporting a saner grade.

From Lake Whatcom Park's upper trailhead the trail for Stewart takes off to the left. You want to follow the gated Wickersham Truck Trail to the right, steadily ascending through a patchwork of old cuts, maturing timber, and the powerline swath. Of course, it's when the trail is climbing up the swath that you'll be inundated with views—and direct sunlight, so don't forget the sunscreen.

The trail makes a few sweeping turns where trails primarily used by mountain bikers branch off. At 0.8 mile, reach the swath for the first time—and views. They only get better as you put away the miles and accumulate elevation. At 1.4 miles, Lookout Mountain comes into view across Lake Whatcom. Lookout is the centerpiece of the reconveyed parcel on the lake's west shore.

Soon pass through a patch of attractive second growth. At 2.3 miles (elev. 2050 feet), just beyond the tower signed "line 1 mile 43 tower 2," the trail from the parking lot—here part of a tower access track—comes in from the left. If you choose to follow it, it's best to take this 2.1-mile trail up and not down, due to some insanely steep sections. The Wickersham Truck Road continues climbing—and your destination peak is now visible.

At 2.7 miles, bear right at a junction, staying on the main road. Old roads to the left can be taken for a loop to the summit, but they are difficult to follow. The main road, however, is a straight shot. Enjoy sweeping views before reentering forest. At 3.7 miles, cross a creek and reach the park's boundary. Here the Wickersham Truck Road continues straight all the way to Wickersham.

You want to take the old logging road (no. 4090) left and follow it across the powerline swath (ignore utility service road spurs). Climbing, enjoy views east to Mount Baker and the Twin Sisters. At 4 miles, bear left at a Y-junction. The way right is overgrown, but you can follow it a short distance for some good views.

Your route enters a patch of hemlocks and firs before popping out at a powerline opening (elev. 2800 feet) at 4.3 miles. The views here across Lake Whatcom are supreme. Locate the Olympics, Mount Erie on Fidalgo Island, Mount Vernon's Little Mountain, Blanchard Mountain, Boundary Bay, Padilla Bay, the Skagit Flats, Lummi Island, Salt Spring Island, Saturna Island—and more!

If you want to continue higher, follow a trail taking off in the woods to the right for 0.2 mile. It ends at a slash pile and limited view just below the 2985-foot summit of this knoll on Stewart Mountain. Stewart's actual summit is much farther north and 100 feet higher. It's on DNR lands and it may soon someday have a trail leading to it as well. Now prepare for a knee-knocking descent.

24 Hovander Homestead and Tennant Lake Parks

DISTANCE:	4 miles of trails
ELEVATION GAIN:	20 feet
HIGH POINT:	25 feet
DIFFICULTY:	Easy
FITNESS:	Hikers, walkers, and runners
FAMILY-FRIENDLY:	Yes, and jogging stroller–friendly
DOG-FRIENDLY:	On- and off-leash areas
AMENITIES:	Privies, water, picnic tables, interpretive centers and displays, lookout tower
CONTACT/MAP:	Washington Department of Fish and Wildlife , Whatcom County Parks and Recreation
GPS:	N 48° 49.851" W 122° 35.585"

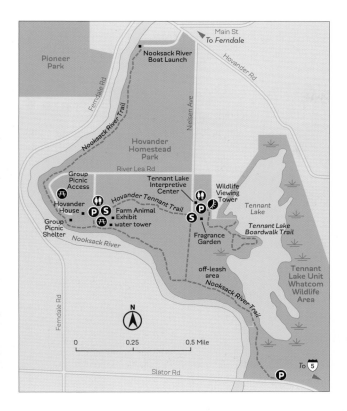

GETTING THERE

Driving: From Bellingham, follow I-5 north to exit 262 in Ferndale. Then head west on Main Street for 0.5 mile. Turn sharply left onto Hovander Road; after 0.1 mile, turn right onto Nielsen Avenue. Continue for 0.7 mile and turn right onto River Lea Road. Proceed for 0.6 mile to the trailhead at the Hovander Homestead main parking area.

Transit: Whatcom Transit Route 27 to Ferndale stops on Main Street close to Hovander River Walk.

Trail through Hovander Homestead farm

Explore nearly 1000 acres of wildlife- and history-rich grounds within the adjacent Hovander Homestead and Tennant Lake parks. Four miles of level trails traverse these two sprawling parcels on the Nooksack River floodplain just south of downtown Ferndale. Run along the glacier-fed river or walk quietly on a boardwalk along Tennant Lake's marshy shores. Combine your exercise and nature jaunts with visits to the parks' lovely gardens and historic homes and farm. Children will especially enjoy Hovander's playground and farmyard animals.

GET MOVING

From the main parking area, walk through the Hovander Homestead to access the trails. The homestead was established in 1898 by Swedish architect Hakan Hovander. Hovander left Sweden for America in 1865 but returned to Sweden to study architecture before returning to America to raise his family. The 6800-square-foot home with gingerbread molding along its exterior eaves was completed in 1903. The barn, one of the largest in the county, was completed several years later. In 1969 the homestead became a Whatcom County Park, and it is listed on the National Register of Historic Places. Tours are conducted in the summer, but you can wander the grounds anytime. Now choose your trail.

NOOKSACK RIVER TRAIL

This trail, also known as the Hovander River Walk, runs on a dike alongside the Nooksack River for 2.4 miles. From the Water Tower Picnic Area, it is 1.2 miles north, primarily through fields, to Main Street. And it's 1.2 miles south to Slater Road through riparian forest and field edges. Both directions make for great walking, running, and hiking, and there is virtually no elevation change.

Southbound, the trail reaches a junction after about 0.4 mile. Here a connector trail leads north 0.4 mile to the Tennant Lake Interpretive Center (described shortly). The Nooksack River Trail continues south here, soon entering Tennant Lake Park, which is managed by the Washington Department of Fish and Wildlife. The trail is leash free here. So let your buddy roam, but be sure to keep her under voice command. The entire Nooksack River Trail is part of the Nooksack Loop Trail, a 45-mile trail being built by the Whatcom Parks and Recreation Foundation, connecting Ferndale, Bellingham, Everson, and Lynden. The Nooksack River Trail reaches a trailhead and parking area (Discover Pass required) at Slater Road. Although the path continues south 2 miles to Marine Drive, it is not maintained and has a lot of muddy and overgrown sections. Only tenacious explorers should consider it until it becomes incorporated into the Nooksack Loop system.

TENNANT LAKE TRAILS

From the Hovander Homestead you can follow the Hovander-Tennant Trail 0.4 mile east along a slough to the Tennant Lake Interpretive Center and Fragrance Garden. Alternatively, you can drive to this spot via Nielsen Avenue and park (Discover Pass required). You can make a nice short loop by taking a 0.4-mile trail that heads south to the Nooksack Trail and following that path west 0.4 mile back to the homestead.

The biggest draw here, however, is the observation tower and 1-mile boardwalk loop trail. Climb the 50-foot tower (pretty much your only elevation gain in this hiking area) and take in views of Mount Baker in the distance. Then scan Tennant Lake below for birds. This rich river bottom lake teems with birds year-round, but especially in the autumn and spring. Look for swans and herons. Then head to the recently renovated boardwalk trail and go bird and critter watching at the lake's marshy edge. Note that the boardwalk is closed from early October to mid-January.

If the Interpretive Center is open, check it out. There are hands-on activities for the kids. And be sure to also visit the award-winning Fragrance Garden with its more than 200 plants. The gardens are wheelchair accessible.

GO FARTHER

From the Nooksack River Trail's northern terminus on Main Street, walk west across the river bridge and then walk south on the concrete Centennial River Walk 0.3 mile to Pioneer Park. You can then wander for hours through this interesting city park containing fifteen historic structures that were moved to these grounds over the years. It is one of the best collections of pioneer structures in the Northwest.

25 Point Whitehorn Marine Reserve

DISTANCE:	0.7 mile of trail and nearly 2 miles of beach
ELEVATION GAIN:	100 feet
HIGH POINT:	100 feet
DIFFICULTY:	Easy to moderate
FITNESS:	Hikers
FAMILY-FRIENDLY:	Yes, and the trail is wheelchair accessible
DOG-FRIENDLY:	Dogs prohibited
AMENITIES:	Privy, interpretive signs
CONTACT/MAP:	Whatcom County Parks and Recreation
GPS:	N 48° 53.239" W 122° 46.800"

GETTING THERE

Driving: From Bellingham, follow I-5 north to exit 266. Then drive Grandview Road (State Route 548) west for 8.4 miles. (Note: Stay on Grandview at the traffic circle where SR 548 departs north to follow Blaine Road.) Then turn left onto Koehn Road and proceed 0.4 mile to the trailhead on your left.

Follow a wide trail through a wet forest of big spruces, cedars, and firs along a high coastal bluff. Pause at a series of viewpoints to gaze out across the Strait of Georgia to the San Juan and Gulf islands. Look for eagles perched in bluff top snags. Then descend a staircase to a lonely rocky beach, sheltered from the outside world by rugged bluffs of glacial till. If the tide is low, explore nearly two miles of beach, savoring splendid Salish Sea scenery and watching for marine mammals and pelagic birds.

GET MOVING

Wedged between the Cherry Point refineries and the resort town of Birch Bay is this ecologically important and surprisingly undeveloped stretch of bluff and beach. In 2007, thanks to the Whatcom Land Trust, 54 prime acres of bluff top forest-land was spared from development and made into a reserve. This not only allowed for the development of a top-notch trail but also provided access to the more than 3000 acres of public seabed and tidelands making up the adjacent DNR-managed Cherry Point Aquatic Reserve.

Follow the wide and well-built trail, suitable for wheelchairs and jogging strollers, south into a forest of maples, alders, birches, and mature evergreens. Because the forest floor here is underlain by dense glacial hardpan clays that prevent rainwater percolation, the path can be saturated during the wetter months. No worries, however, as the trail builders constructed many boardwalks over these pools of standing water.

Eventually the trail reaches the rim of the bluff, passing a handful of vista points complete with benches. At 0.75 mile the good trail ends. Now descend a long stairway, reaching

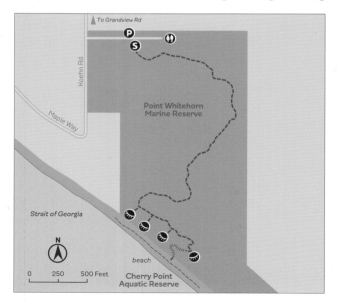

Stairway to shoreline at Point Whitehorn Marine Reserve

the shoreline. If the tide is out, consider some beach walking. You can walk a short way north before reaching private
tidelands, which include Point Whitehorn. So instead, venture
south over cobbled stones and stretches of clay. The walking
can be slow and cumbersome—all the more reason to pause
and watch for wildlife along the way. You can walk 1.6 miles,

all the way to the Cherry Point refinery's tanker pier. Opened in 1971, the Cherry Point refinery was the last major refinery built in the country. Recently this area was being considered for the controversial Gateway Pacific Terminal, a super-port for coal exports. But in May 2016 the Army Corp of Engineers denied a permit to the project, primarily to honor the Lummi Nation's treaty-protected fishing rights.

GO FARTHER
Head over to nearby Birch Bay State Park (Discover Pass required) for some much easier beach walking on sandy shoreline. Check out the 0.5-mile Terrell Marsh Interpretive Trail within the 194-acre park.

26 Semiahmoo Spit

DISTANCE:	0.8 mile of trail and 1 mile of beach
ELEVATION GAIN:	10 feet
HIGH POINT:	10 feet
DIFFICULTY:	Easy
FITNESS:	Walkers and runners
FAMILY-FRIENDLY:	Yes, and the trail is wheelchair accessible
DOG-FRIENDLY:	On leash
AMENITIES:	Privy, water, picnic shelter, historic structures, interpretive signs
CONTACT/MAP:	Whatcom County Parks and Recreation
GPS:	N 48° 58.675" W 122° 47.529"

GETTING THERE
Driving: From Bellingham, follow I-5 north to exit 274. Take a right onto Peace Portal Drive, then immediately turn left onto State Route 548 (Bell Road, which becomes Blaine Road). Drive 1 mile and turn right onto Drayton Road. Continue for 0.9 mile, bearing right onto Drayton Harbor Road. Then drive 2.4 miles and turn right onto the Semiahmoo Parkway.

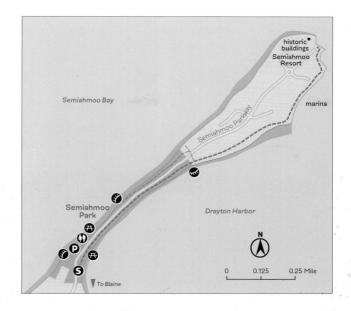

Proceed for 0.4 mile, turning left into the Semiahmoo Park parking area and trailhead.

It's your choice—a paved trail along Drayton Harbor sporting breathtaking views of Mount Baker or a sandy, rocky beach along Boundary Bay granting glimpses of snowy British Columbia peaks hovering above White Rock and South Surrey. The birding is exceptional on both sides of the narrow spit. And there are plenty of historical points of interest on both ends of the spit. Best you see it all, making a loop on this protruding piece of land just south of the international border.

GET MOVING

The Semiahmoo Spit was once home to a massive Alaska Packers Association (APA) cannery, the largest cannery in the country. You can learn about it at the county park. And

Mount Baker makes a stunning backdrop for Drayton Harbor.

at the far end of the spit, where an upscale resort now stands, you can roam around, checking out some of the remaining APA buildings and structures from the cannery days.

History buffs will no doubt love this location—so too will birders. Both Drayton Harbor and Semiahmoo Bay host thousands of migratory birds each fall and spring. One of the largest concentrations of loons I have ever seen in the Pacific Northwest was at the mouth of Drayton Harbor. Watch for plovers, dunlins, eagles, herons, and brants too. And every March the area is host to the Wings over Water Northwest Birding Festival.

From the parking area, carefully cross the Semiahmoo Parkway and reach the park's paved trail. It's part of the Coast

Millennium Trail, a trail in progress that is planned to some-day span Whatcom County's shoreline from Blaine to Larra-bee State Park. The route heads left here. However, you can hike right too if you'd like—the trail leads uphill into a nicely laid out and landscaped development.

The trail parallels the road, which normally would be a dis-traction—but your attention will be captured by Mount Baker and the Twin Sisters, beyond Drayton Harbor. At 0.8 mile, the trail enters the Semiahmoo Resort. Here you can continue straight on the resort's paths to the marina, historic buildings, docks, and the spit's iconic old water tower.

For the return, you can locate a trail at the park/resort boundary, cutting across the spit to the Semiahmoo Bay side. Here you can follow a trail on the spit or walk the beach. Just be sure you do *not* take any trails posted by the resort for guests only. Now enjoy excellent views across Boundary Bay to Point Roberts and BC's Gulf Islands, and across Semiah-moo Bay to White Rock and South Surrey in BC. Look to the northeast and locate the distinctive Golden Ears mountains. And keep your eyes on the water for seals and all kinds of avian activity. When the tide is out, the beach walking is won-derful here. Once you return to the parking area, you can con-tinue a little farther south on more public tidelands if you like.

GO FARTHER

From the tip of the spit you can take a passenger ferry (from Memorial Day to Labor Day) across the mouth of Drayton Harbor to the Blaine Harbor Marina. It's via the MV *Plover*, a historic vessel from the 1940s once used to ferry cannery workers. From the marina, head over to Marine Park (also reached by car via Marine Drive off exit 276 on I-5) and walk a mile of paved paths along Semiahmoo Bay. Kids will love the Nautical Playground. Looking for more? Walk a few blocks east to the International Peace Arch Park and wander through manicured gardens straddling the 49th parallel.

27 Berthusen Park

DISTANCE:	7 miles of trails
ELEVATION GAIN:	20 feet
HIGH POINT:	110 feet
DIFFICULTY:	Easy
FITNESS:	Walkers, runners, and hikers
FAMILY-FRIENDLY:	Yes
DOG-FRIENDLY:	On leash
AMENITIES:	Privy, picnic shelter, playground, historic structures
CONTACT/MAP:	City of Lynden Parks
GPS:	N 48° 57.771" W 122° 30.591"

GETTING THERE

Driving: From Bellingham, take exit 256A off of I-5 and head north on State Route 539 (Meridian Street). Continue for 11.3 miles to Lynden, turning left onto West Main Street. Then drive 0.9 mile, turning right onto Berthusen Road. Proceed 1.1 miles and turn left into Berthusen Park. Continue 0.2 mile to parking at the picnic area and trailhead.

Homesteaded in 1883 by Norwegian immigrant Hans Berthusen, this wonderful 236-acre tract became a park in 1944 when Hans and his wife, Lida, willed it to the people of Lynden. The beautiful, large barn that still stands here was constructed from trees on the property. And a towering tract of old growth still stands on this homestead as well. Take to the park's trails and explore these ancient trees as well as old structures and babbling Berthusen Creek.

GET MOVING

Trails take off everywhere from the park's picnic and play areas. Some are marked; some aren't. But it matters not, as this park is made for aimless wandering. Except for where Berthusen Creek cuts through the property, the park's grounds

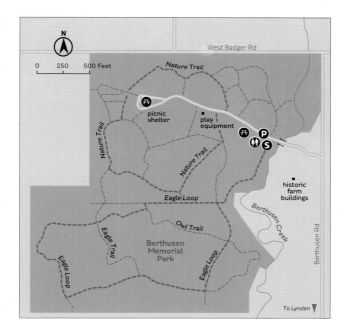

are nearly level. If you like, you can study the map at the kiosk near the first picnic shelter—then hit the trails.

South of the access road you can follow a single track along winding Berthusen Creek or a wider trail (an old woods road) on the bench above the creek for about 0.2 mile to the start of the Eagle Loop. Developed by Eagle Scouts, this delightful trail loops 1.1 miles through the southern reaches of the park, primarily through uniform, mature second-growth conifers. There are several trails that branch off from it leading to the edge of the property—abruptly defined by farmland against this heavily forested tract. The 0.2-mile Eagle Trail and 0.25-mile Owl Trail connect portions of the loop, allowing for some figure-eight hiking.

Old-growth forest in Berthusen Park

The real treat in this park is the 0.8-mile Nature Trail, which starts just north of the first picnic shelter. It immediately enters the Berthusen Grove, a 20-acre tract of towering primeval forest. How it survived among all of the surrounding cleared land for agriculture is quite remarkable. Berthusen wanted to keep a remnant tract of virgin timber as a testament to what this area looked like upon his arrival. According to the Lynden Parks Department, Berthusen refused to cut this timber (and it was worth a considerable amount), saying the money couldn't compensate for the pride and pleasure he derived from living among these big old trees. You'll appreciate walking among them. And you'll enjoy checking out some of the other trails leading from this old-growth grove as well.

GO FARTHER

From Lynden City Park on Depot Road, pick up the paved Jim Kaemingk Sr. Trail and follow it (with a short residential road section) for about 1.5 miles along Fishtrap Creek to the Lynden Bender Fields. It's a lovely running and walking route through this quaint Whatcom County city that was heavily settled by Dutch immigrants in the early 20th century.

Next page: *Dunlins feeding in Padilla Bay
with Mount Baker in the background*

SKAGIT VALLEY

One of the last large greenbelts remaining between Seattle and Vancouver, BC, the Skagit Valley is known and cherished for its farms and tulip fields and its wintering flocks of snow geese and swans. The river that defines and gives its name to the valley is one of the Northwest's mightiest and least developed. Draining the third largest watershed on the American West Coast, the Skagit is also the only major river in Washington harboring healthy populations of all five native salmon species. Gateway to both the San Juan Islands and North Cascades, the lower Skagit Valley—home to the small cities of Mount Vernon, Burlington, and Sedro-Woolley—also contains an array of fine parks and preserves with miles of trails.

28 Padilla Bay Dike Trail

DISTANCE:	4.8 miles roundtrip
ELEVATION GAIN:	30 feet
HIGH POINT:	30 feet
DIFFICULTY:	Easy
FITNESS:	Hikers, walkers, and runners
FAMILY-FRIENDLY:	Yes, wide, level, smooth soft-surface trail suitable for jogging strollers, but be aware that adjacent bay lands are open to waterfowl hunting in season
DOG-FRIENDLY:	On leash
AMENITIES:	Benches, privies, interpretive signs
CONTACT/MAP:	Padilla Bay National Estuarine Research Reserve, Skagit County Parks and Recreation
GPS:	N 48 28.818 W 122 28.383

GETTING THERE

Driving: From Burlington (exit 231 on I-5), proceed through roundabouts and head west on Josh Wilson Road for 6.4 miles. Upon entering the village of Bay View, turn left onto 2nd Street and continue for 0.1 mile to the Skagit County Historical Society's large parking area. Park here for the trail.

Take to a well-groomed and well-loved trail atop a snaking dike built by tenacious 20th-century settlers and farmers. The way winds through the Padilla Bay National Estuarine Research Reserve. Established in 1980 to protect extensive mudflats of eelgrass, the 11,000-acre reserve is a birder's paradise. The trail twists and turns along sloughs, tidal flats, and salt marshes, allowing you to scope out herons, eagles, falcons, dunlins, brants, and scores of other winged residents. And aside from the profuse birdlife, you'll be treated to unhindered views of Mount Baker, the San Juan Islands, and active farmlands from this delightful and level path.

Indian Slough at Padilla Bay National Estuarine Research Reserve

GET MOVING

Begin by walking south on 2nd Street to Bayview-Edison Road. Then carefully walk east along this road, coming to the Padilla Bay Shore Trailhead at 0.15 mile. The short drop in elevation from parking lot to trailhead is the only elevation change you'll experience on this trail. Now relax and enjoy this perfectly level trail for the next 2.25 miles.

Developed in 1990 through the cooperation of a consortium of public agencies, the Padilla Bay Shore Trail allows the best pedestrian viewings of the estuarine reserve. Established for research, education, and stewardship, Padilla is one of only twenty-eight such reserves in the country. And while Padilla harbors some of the best remaining eelgrass flats north of Willapa Bay, the area has been heavily influenced by agriculture and industry. Farmers have reclaimed thousands of acres of tide flats for croplands, and two large oil refineries operate across the bay at March Point.

SKAGIT VALLEY IBA

Northwest beer connoisseurs are well aware of IPAs. And Northwest birders are quite familiar with IBAs—Important Bird Areas. Established by Birdlife International (founded in 1922 as the International Committee for Bird Protection), a global partnership of conservation groups concerned about protecting birds and their habitats, IBAs are of global importance in protecting bird populations. The Skagit Valley contains two large IBAs: Skagit Bay and Samish/Padilla Bays.

These two areas are home to a myriad of resident species and host to thousands of migratory birds, including trumpeter and tundra swans, snow geese, and brants. According to the Skagit Audubon Society, it is thought that the entire population—about 20,000—of the western high arctic brant (a species or subspecies—taxonomists change their minds—also known as grey-bellied brant) winters in the eelgrass-rich waters of Padilla Bay. The Padilla and Samish bays also support large raptor populations, including gyrfalcons. Snowy owls occasionally frequent the grassy shores of these bays as well.

Skagit Bay provides prime habitat for thousands of wintering lesser snow geese, tundra swans, and trumpeter swans. The Skagit Delta hosts the largest concentrations of wintering trumpeter swans in the country. The delta also sees upward of 60,000 wintering snow geese from Russia's Wrangel Island—the last major breeding population in Asia. More than 30,000 dunlins also winter at Skagit Bay. Boundary Bay in Whatcom County and British Columbia is another great spot for viewing wintering dunlins and other shorebirds.

The Skagit Valley is also well known for its wintering bald eagles (as well as year-round residents). Hundreds of eagles from Alaska come to the river from November to February to feast on salmon carcasses. Whatcom County's Nooksack River and Boundary Bay are also

But the area still remains ecologically viable and incredibly scenic, especially during low tide, when nearly the entire 8- by 3-mile bay is transformed into glistening mudflats and slithering sloughs. Hordes of herons harvesting succulent appetizers can often be observed. Be sure to shift your attention to the neighboring "drier" grounds for songbird and raptor observations.

Trumpeter swans are welcome visitors to Skagit Valley fields and skies.

wintering eagle hot spots. And Padilla Bay is home to one of the largest great blue heron rookeries in the western half of the country. Although this rookery (protected by the Skagit Land Trust) on March Point, which contains over 700 active nests, is off-limits for visitors, herons can be spotted all over the bay.

The best birding spots in this book include Clayton Beach (Trail 16), Point Whitehorn Marine Reserve (Trail 25), Semiahmoo Spit (Trail 26), Padilla Bay Dike Trail (Trail 28), Skagit Wildlife Area (Trail 30), Cascade Trail (Trail 34), Kiket Island (Trail 35), and the Tommy Thompson Trail (Trail 36).

But if birding ruffles your feathers, the surrounding scenery should still tickle your fancy. Islands dot the bay. Across Padilla, the conifer-cloaked knolls of Sugarloaf and Mount Erie crown Fidalgo Island. Mount Baker rises above the foothills to the east, and to the south, far beyond the Skagit Flats, looms Mount Rainier.

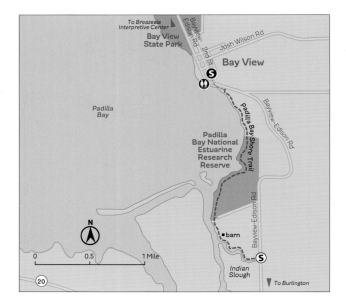

At 1.8 miles you'll approach a slough-side barn, a favorite motif among photographers, casual and serious alike. The trail now turns away from the mudflats, following a snaking Indian Slough for its final half mile, terminating at its southern trailhead on the Bayview-Edison Road. From this alternative starting area (parking is limited), begin your return, enjoying a new phase of the bay.

GO FARTHER

Visit the Preserve's Breazeale Interpretive Center, located on the Bayview-Edison Road 1.2 miles north of the trail-head. Here you'll also find a kid-friendly 0.8-mile nature trail through preserve uplands and a short paved trail leading to an observation deck on the bay. Nearby Bay View State Park, with its cozy campsites and cabins, makes for a great excuse to stay overnight.

29 Skagit Airport Trails

DISTANCE:	Up to 10.1 miles of trails
ELEVATION GAIN:	Up to 140 feet
HIGH POINT:	160 feet
DIFFICULTY:	Easy
FITNESS:	Walkers and runners
FAMILY-FRIENDLY:	Yes, and jogging stroller–friendly
DOG-FRIENDLY:	On leash
AMENITIES:	Privy
CONTACT/MAP:	Port of Skagit, Be Active Skagit
GPS:	N 48° 27.469' W 122° 24.844"

GETTING THERE

Driving: From Bellingham, follow I-5 south to exit 230 in Burlington. Then follow State Route 20 west for 3.5 miles, turning right onto Higgins Airport Way. Proceed north for 0.5 mile to the trailhead, on your left at the junction with Ovenell Road.

Transit: Skagit Transit (SKAT) Route 513 (weekdays)

Looking for a wonderful network of family-friendly walking and running trails in the Skagit Valley? Consider the airport! Back in 2000, the Port of Skagit came up with a plan to build a trail network throughout much of the lands adjacent to the airport. Great plan—and don't worry about the planes, as this is a quiet regional airport. Instead, enjoy birds in flight and the croaking of frogs while cruising these well-manicured trails. And you can keep your shoes on here!

GET MOVING

There are more than 10 miles of trail to walk and run here, and numerous loops can be made to cater to your exercise desires. In general, the trails south of the airstrips are in a more natural setting, cutting through wetlands and groves of big maples and towering cottonwoods. The trails north of the airstrips parallel port roads and pass by businesses. All of the trails are wide and soft surface and are suitable for jogging strollers. Some of the trails can be wet and prone to minor flooding during fall and winter rainy periods.

From the main trailhead you can (carefully) cross Ovenell Road and explore 0.5 mile of rarely used trail going through meadows usually teeming with birds and other critters. Enjoy good views here too of Cultus Mountain to the east. The trail leading west from the main parking area parallels Ovenell Road and connects to other trails, where you can make a

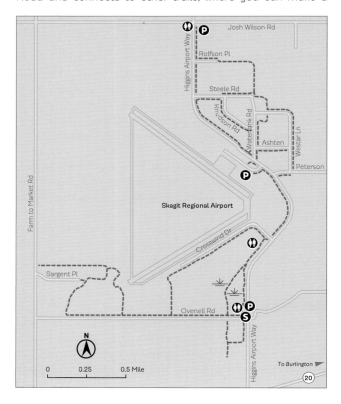

Running on the Skagit Airport Trails

2.9-mile lollipop loop west—or a 2.1-mile loop north. The trail running parallel with the main trail traveling north along Higgins Airport Way cuts through a wetland.

You can continue on the trail paralleling Higgins Airport Way and cross Crosswind Drive. Then run or walk 0.6 mile along the airport periphery, enjoying good views of the foothills to the east. Cross Higgins Airport Way and continue on the main trail 0.9 mile to Josh Wilson Road, where there is also parking and a privy. You can also make some loops here in the northern reaches of the trail system. While the area is in essence an industrial park, it is light industry, not too busy, and on weekends and weeknights pretty quiet. This is one of my favorite local running spots, so maybe I'll see you out there.

30 Skagit Wildlife Area: Headquarters Unit

DISTANCE:	1.9 miles of trails
ELEVATION GAIN:	10 feet
HIGH POINT:	5 feet
DIFFICULTY:	Easy
FITNESS:	Walkers and hikers
FAMILY-FRIENDLY:	Yes, and partially jogging stroller–friendly
DOG-FRIENDLY:	On leash
AMENITIES:	Privy
CONTACT/MAP:	Washington Department of Fish and Wildlife (WDFW)
GPS:	N 48° 19.537" W 122° 22.770"
BEFORE YOU GO:	A Discover Pass or WDFW Vehicle Access Pass is required.

GETTING THERE

Driving: From Bellingham and Mount Vernon, follow I-5 south to exit 221 in Conway. Turn right and proceed to the traffic circle. Then continue west on Fir Island Road for 1.7 miles, turning left onto Wylie Road. Proceed 1.1 miles, entering the Headquarters Unit of the Skagit Wildlife Area. Then turn right on Game Farm Road, reaching the trailhead and parking in 0.1 mile.

This is a popular walking spot for Skagit Valley residents and one of the best birding locations in Washington; you won't have to exert much energy walking on these nearly level paths. Walk along Wiley Slough and Freshwater Slough at the mouth of the South Fork of the Skagit River on Skagit Bay, looking for swans, geese, herons, eagles, songbirds, and countless raptors, waders, and dabblers. And admire Mount Baker acting as a snowy backdrop to fields flush with thousands of snow geese.

GET MOVING

While the Skagit Wildlife Area is a popular birding area—particularly for wintering Wrangel Island snow geese—it is also an active hunting area in season. The best time to visit is right after snow goose hunting season ends (usually in late January) and before the geese return to Alaska (usually by April). If you choose to visit during hunting season, be sure to wear orange and stay on the trails. The Skagit Wildlife Area consists of nearly 17,000 acres in several parcels primarily within the Skagit River Delta. This section, the Headquarters Unit (home to the refuge's offices), is the best in the refuge for walking and hiking.

From the parking area, walk a few hundred feet back on the road, coming to the trailhead on a levee. Now turn right (you can walk left, too, if you'd like, a short distance to a boat launch) and walk the wide levee. Come to a junction at 0.3 mile.

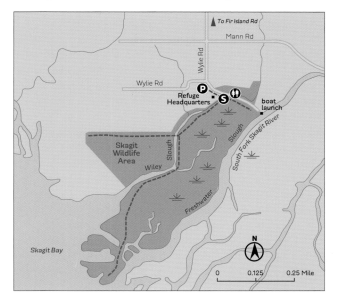

Flooded field at Skagit Wildlife Area

The main wide levee trail continues right, soon crossing Wiley Slough. Follow it for 0.5 mile to its end. Here a trail once led left on a levee to form a loop, but it was breached years ago for salt marsh restoration. Before retracing your steps, look north over the fields. Here, from late fall through early spring, thousands of snow geese can often be seen. Get out your telephoto lens. When they take to the air, their wild clamor is sure to get your attention.

The other unit trail is a little more primitive and not suited for jogging strollers. Follow it along Wiley Slough and extensive wetlands and marshes. Scan the reeds, bulrushes, grasses, and snags here for a myriad of bird species. Enjoy good views too, of Mount Baker towering in the distance.

At 1 mile, the trail ends at the extensive tidal flats lining Skagit Bay. Just to your left, the South Fork Skagit River's Freshwater Slough empties into this wildlife-rich bay. The entire delta here has remained remarkably undeveloped, in sharp contrast to many other Salish Sea river deltas that have succumbed to development. Wildlife officials continue to restore and enhance lands here within the wildlife area and across the Skagit Delta, ensuring quality habitat for the myriad of migratory and resident species here.

GO FARTHER

You can explore a couple of the other nearby units of the Skagit Wildlife Area. South, near Stanwood, find good walking at the Leque Island and Big Ditch units. And north near Edison, the Samish Unit offers a short paved trail to a pond on the flats near Padilla Bay.

31 Mount Vernon Riverwalk

DISTANCE:	2 miles roundtrip
ELEVATION GAIN:	5 feet
HIGH POINT:	30 feet
DIFFICULTY:	Easy
FITNESS:	Walkers and runners
FAMILY-FRIENDLY:	Yes, and jogging stroller–friendly
DOG-FRIENDLY:	On leash
AMENITIES:	Privy, water, benches, sculptures
CONTACT/MAP:	City of Mount Vernon, Mount Vernon Parks and Recreation
GPS:	N 48° 25.578" W 122° 20.351"

GETTING THERE

Driving: From Bellingham, follow I-5 south to exit 227 (College Way). Turn right and immediately turn left onto Freeway Drive. Continue 0.7 mile south to Lions Park and the trailhead on your right.

From downtown Mount Vernon, follow Freeway Drive north for 0.4 mile, turning left into Lions Park.

Transit: Skagit Transit Route 207

Part of the Mount Vernon Waterfront Revitalization and Flood Protection Project, this fairly new pedestrian path along the Skagit River is fast becoming the civic pride of Mount Vernon. Walk along the river that has defined and shaped this small city—the largest in the county and the county seat—taking in historical, natural, and cultural landmarks.

GET MOVING

From the Lions Park parking area you can walk north on a soft surface path paralleling Freeway Drive and the Skagit River to a wooded section of park. Here, follow a recently upgraded trail through a grove of towering cottonwoods at a bend in the river. The trail ends in 0.4 mile at a small parking area on the corner of Riverbend Road and Freeway Drive.

The concrete Riverwalk heads south, passing a play field and hugging a bank of the Skagit River. As you approach downtown Mount Vernon, notice the old stack to the left adorned with a big tulip. Mount Vernon and the Skagit Valley

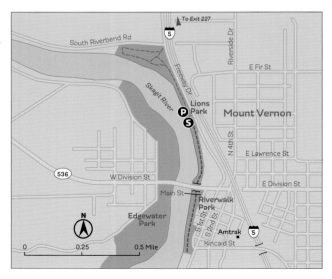

Running along the Skagit River on the Mount Vernon Riverwalk

are known throughout the region for their tulip fields and Tulip Festival held throughout April. During that period, either come for the festivities or avoid the crowds.

The way dips under Division Street and enters the Skagit Riverwalk Park. Until a decade ago this whole area was an old revetment and parking lot. Today it's a wonderful riverside downtown park that hosts events, markets, downtown workers on lunch break, and tourists out for a stroll. Enjoy the sculptures, particularly the Tulip Dance Sculpture. Continue walking, coming to the Riverwalk's end at 0.6 mile just south of Kincaid Street.

The Riverwalk will eventually be extended another 0.4 mile to the city's water treatment plant. Many area residents, including this author, hope that this trail is the beginning of what will someday become an extended trail system on the Skagit River's dikes—similar to the excellent systems in place in the Tri-Cities and Lewiston-Clarkston.

For now, retrace your steps or divert to downtown for a drink or something to eat.

GO FARTHER

From Lions Park, cross Freeway Drive and follow the wide walkway 0.3 mile along Cameron Way, which merges into Fir Street, to the junction with Riverside Drive. Then cross Riverside Drive and locate the Kulshan Trail at the rear of the Skagit Habitat for Humanity shop. Now run or walk this paved trail for 2.1 miles through a forested corridor and Bakerview Park all the way to its end at Waugh Road. Koma Kulshan was the Native American name for Mount Baker, and you'll see this mountain from the popular trail.

In nearby Burlington you can walk or run 1.5 miles along the Skagit River on a dike-top trail at the city's Skagit River Park (access off of Skagit Street). Another pleasant, albeit short, trail to check out in Burlington is the new paved Tammi Wilson Memorial Trail, which leaves busy Burlington Boulevard near the Cascade Mall (park there) to follow alongside Gages Slough—a natural patch remaining within this commercial zone. It dips under I-5, ending on Goldenrod Road.

32 Little Mountain Park

DISTANCE:	More than 10 miles of trail
ELEVATION GAIN:	Up to 600 feet
HIGH POINT:	934 feet
DIFFICULTY:	Easy to difficult
FITNESS:	Walkers, runners, and hikers
FAMILY-FRIENDLY:	Yes, but be aware that some trails see heavy mountain bike use
DOG-FRIENDLY:	On leash
AMENITIES:	Privy, benches, picnic tables, overlooks
CONTACT/MAP:	City of Mount Vernon, Mount Vernon Parks and Recreation
GPS:	N 48° 24.079" W 122° 18.248"

GETTING THERE

Driving: From Bellingham or Mount Vernon, follow I-5 south to exit 225. Then head east on Anderson Road (which becomes LaVenture Road) for 1 mile. Then turn right onto Blackburn Road. Drive 0.3 mile and bear right onto Little Mountain Road. Continue for 0.4 mile, turning right onto the 1.4-mile park road and parking (elev. 400 feet); more parking is available about midway and at the road's end on Little Mountain Summit. For the East Trailhead (elev. 350 feet), drive past the main park entrance for 0.5 mile to parking on your right.

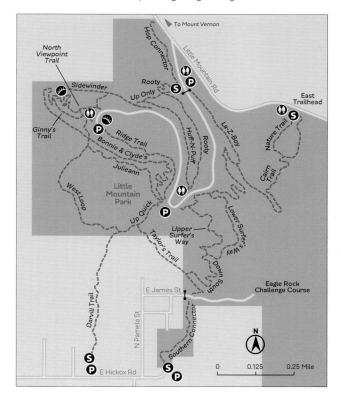

Mount Vernon's grand park, thickly forested Little Mountain rises more than 900 feet above the farmlands of the Skagit River delta. Devoted volunteers have worked hard (and continue to do so) building and maintaining an excellent network of trails exceeding 10 miles on the park's sprawling 522 acres. Walk, run, or hike through impressive forest groves, along a peaceful creek, and to two overlooks providing sweeping views of Mount Vernon, Mount Baker, the Olympic Mountains, and a checkerboard of tulip farms and agricultural lands below.

GET MOVING
Little Mountain Park's several trailheads and extensive trail system allow for many loops and variations. Be sure to download a map before you go as it's easy to end up on the opposite side of the mountain from where you began. Of course, if that's intentional you're sure to get a great workout. This park is a favorite for local trail runners (including this author) training for races. The park is also popular with area mountain bikers, so stay alert when hiking with dogs and children. However, there are several hiker-only trails within the park.

For easier rambling, consider the jogging stroller–friendly Nature Trail and Sidekick from the East Trailhead. This 0.5-mile loop, along with the North Viewpoint Loop Trail also host Poetry in the Park, where you'll be greeted with signs displaying poetry by local poets (in English *y Español tambien*) and children.

The 0.5-mile Cairn Trail leaves this loop, traversing mature stands of conifers and maples and connecting with the La-Z-Boy Trail. You can head right on this trail to the trailhead at the park's entrance or head left on it to the Over the Top Trail, leading to trails to the mountain's summit. Here, cross the park road and continue to the summit via the hiker-only Ridge, Julieann, and Fred's trails. From the East Trailhead to the summit via these trails, plan on distances from 1.6 to 2 miles one-way.

North Lookout

Once on the summit, absolutely visit both of the lookouts. The one on the mountain's high point offers sweeping views west across the Skagit flats to the Olympics. It is stunning during sunsets. The north lookout can be found by following the North Viewpoint Trail 0.1 mile. Here look out over the city of Mount Vernon to Mount Baker.

On the park's southern reaches you can drive to two trail-heads (elev. 80 feet), with parking on Hickox Road (reached from Cedardale Road, accessed from I-5 off of either exit 224 or 225). Here you have the choice of several much longer trails to the summit, including a couple of hiker-only trails, which are generally much quieter than those from the north side.

Hike or run 1.2 miles on the shared-with-bikes Southern Connector, Down South, and Upper Surfer's Way to the park road, where you can continue on the 0.4-mile Ridge Trail to the summit. The Darvill Trail—named for Fred Darvill, a long-time Mount Vernon conservationist and guidebook author (who first introduced me to the North Cascades)—crosses land donated to the Skagit Land Trust by Fred's widow and fellow conservationist, Ginny Darvill. Follow this hiker-only trail through mature woods 0.55 mile to a junction. Then go right on hiker-only Up Quick for 0.2 mile; from here, you can follow either the Ridge Trail or the 0.4-mile Julieann and 0.1-mile Fred's Trail to the summit. Or go left on the more challenging 0.5-mile West Loop Trail and the 0.1 mile Fred's Trail to the summit.

There are so many variations you can do here that you could easily spend a couple of days racking up some serious mileage. The all-volunteer Mount Vernon Trail builders continue to add trails to the park's system—so don't be surprised to find a new one on a return visit.

33 Northern State Recreation Area

DISTANCE:	More than 5 miles of trails
ELEVATION GAIN:	Up to 150 feet
HIGH POINT:	200 feet
DIFFICULTY:	Easy
FITNESS:	Hikers, walkers, and runners
FAMILY-FRIENDLY:	Yes, but be aware that trails shared with mountain bikers and equestrians
DOG-FRIENDLY:	On leash
AMENITIES:	Benches, privy, disc golf course, interpretive signs, picnic tables
CONTACT/MAP:	Skagit County Parks and Recreation
GPS:	N 48° 31.727" W 122° 11.724"

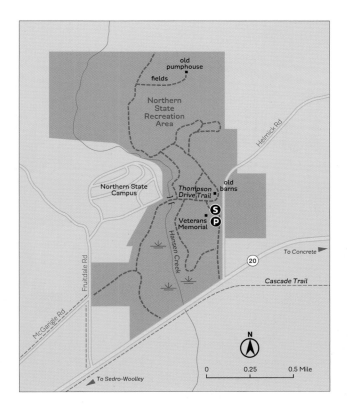

GETTING THERE

Driving: From Bellingham, follow I-5 south to exit 232, then drive Cook Road 4.3 miles east to State Route 20. Go through the roundabout and continue 2.8 miles east on SR 20, turning left onto Helmick Road. Then continue 0.4 mile, turning left into the parking area for the trailhead.

From Burlington (exit 230 on I-5), follow SR 20 east for 8 miles, turning left onto Helmick Road. Then continue 0.4 mile, turning left into the parking area for the trailhead.

Running through the old Northern State Hospital farm grounds

Wander on old roads, now quiet, grassy trails through what was once a large dairy farm for the historically significant Northern State Hospital. Farming ceased in the 1970s, and 723 acres of the hospital farm became a Skagit County park. There's plenty of history here, with barns dating back to the 1920s. And there's a lot of natural wonders here too, with a salmon-rearing creek, sprawling wetland meadows, quiet, secluded fields, and some big trees. The area is full of mystique, too, including claims of hauntings, adding a little excitement to your adventuring.

GET MOVING

The large, yellow barns on a bluff north of the trailhead are probably what will first grab your attention on your drive into the park. In 1909, the Northern State Hospital was built just to the west. It was designed by the Massachusetts-based Olmsted Brothers, an influential landscape architectural firm responsible for designing many highly acclaimed projects— among them Portland, Oregon's, and Seattle's park systems, as well as scenic drives in Acadia, Yosemite, and Great Smoky Mountains national parks.

The hospital treated patients with mental illnesses and was generally regarded as one of the better facilities in the country at the time. It had its own farm, worked by the patients, providing necessities such as food and clothing. After the hospital closed, the farm became a park while the hospital grounds and buildings, with their beautiful Spanish Colonial Revival architecture, provided office and facility space for several operations. It is closed to the public and is currently being assessed for rehabilitation and new uses.

There is plenty to explore here, but stay out of all buildings since they are historic landmarks and unsafe due to deteriorating conditions. The main trail starts at the Veterans Memorial and leads north 0.15 mile to a junction with an old road, once part of Thompson Drive. Head to the right here, passing the old barns and milking operation, and continue north 0.5 mile, where a nice 0.6-mile loop can be made right in pastures and by an old barn.

You can also continue on an old road-trail west, passing the old slaughterhouse. The trail—lined with horse chestnuts (a European import), big Douglas firs, and one gigantic cottonwood—descends toward Hansen Creek. Along the way two trails depart left, traversing the popular disc golf course and returning to the Thompson Drive Trail in 0.35 mile. If you're looking for solitude—and perhaps a bear (be aware) and elk (especially in the winter months)—continue toward the creek. Here a bridge once stood, as the road once went to the Northern State Hospital. Go right here on another former farm road, now a trail.

Follow this grassy path lined with Himalayan blackberry bushes (invasive, but its berries are loved by birds, bears, and hikers), slowly ascending and passing more farm structures falling into disrepair. At 0.55 mile, reach a junction. From here you can continue straight 0.15 mile to the trail's end in a grove of alders. Better yet, take the path right, passing along a field edge granting good views of Lyman Hill looming above. This path ends in 0.3 mile at the old pump house—which indeed looks like it belongs in a 1970s horror flick.

Several more trails can be accessed from the old Thompson Drive Trail. These trails, leading to the park's western and southern reaches, contrast with the park's northern section. Here much of the terrain is wetland meadow and restored Hansen Creek floodplain. The paths are elevated, and they usually stay dry.

Follow one path east of Hansen Creek 0.5 mile across open terrain, gaining good views of the Cascade foothills standing watch over the Skagit Valley. This path connects to another one, which parallels Helmick Road. You can head south on this trail 0.3 mile to SR 20. Carefully cross the busy road and then continue your hike or run on the Cascade Trail (Trail 34).

Continue west on Thompson Drive Trail, coming to a sturdy new bridge spanning Hansen Creek. Then proceed 0.5 mile to a junction. The way right traverses wide, grassy, marshy meadows flush with birds and summer irises. It terminates in 0.35 mile on Fruitdale Road. The way south continues across marshy meadows, granting excellent views of surrounding peaks, terminating in 0.45 mile at SR 20. These paths tend to be lightly traveled, so enjoy the solitude.

GO FARTHER

From the trail ending on Fruitdale Road you can take a paved path paralleling Fruitdale Road for 0.4 mile south to SR 20 near the trailhead to the Cascade Trail. Follow that trail east 0.9 mile to the trailhead at the junction of Helmick Road and SR 20. Carefully cross the busy highway and return by trail to the Northern State parking lot. You can also follow a paved path paralleling McGarigle Road for 0.8 mile west to SR 9 near the North Cascades National Park visitor center.

34 Cascade Trail

DISTANCE:	Up to 22.5 miles
ELEVATION GAIN:	Up to 175 feet
HIGH POINT:	240 feet
DIFFICULTY:	Easy
FITNESS:	Hikers, walkers, and runners
FAMILY-FRIENDLY:	Yes, and the western 0.75 mile is paved and suitable for wheelchairs. The remainder of the trail can accommodate jogging strollers, but spots are bumpy. The trail is also open to bikes and horses.
DOG-FRIENDLY:	On leash
AMENITIES:	Benches, privy
CONTACT/MAP:	Skagit County Parks and Recreation
GPS:	N 48° 30.900" W 122° 12.707"

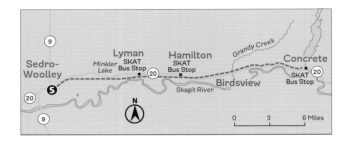

GETTING THERE

Driving: From Bellingham, follow I-5 south to exit 232. Then take Cook Road 4.3 miles east to State Route 20. Go through the roundabout and continue 1.8 miles east on SR 20 to the trailhead (on your right) just before the junction with Fruitdale Road.

From Burlington (exit 230 on I-5), follow SR 20 east for 7 miles to the trailhead (on your right) just before the junction with Fruitdale Road.

Transit: Skagit Transit (SKAT) Route 717 stops at Township Street in Sedro-Woolley, close to the trail's western terminus; in Lyman, near the trail crossing on Main Street; on Petit Street in Hamilton; and in Concrete near the trail's eastern terminus, allowing for one-way runs and hikes.

This railway was once a trunk line of the Great Northern and later Burlington Northern railroads; in 1999, a stretch of more than 22 miles was converted to trail. Beginning in Sedro-Woolley and traveling up the Skagit Valley to Concrete, almost the entire route is in a rural setting. Unlike many rail-trails that cut through backyards and industrial centers, the Cascade Trail traverses mainly farmlands and forest. The western section from Sedro-Woolley to Lyman is the most scenic, traveling through protected wetlands and alongside the Skagit River. It's popular with local runners, and you may see me and members of my running club, the Skagit Runners, out training for upcoming races.

Running through farmland on the Cascade Trail

GET MOVING

The western and eastern ends of the trail are the most inter-esting if you are planning on doing an out-and-back hike or run of various distances. The best one-way option (or long roundtrip) is from Sedro-Woolley to Lyman. Consider car shuttling and transit for one-way trips, including doing the entire trail in one fell swoop. An excellent bakery and pizza parlor in Concrete at trail's end are great incentives for your trip's completion.

From the main trailhead in Sedro-Woolley the Cascade Trail travels west for 0.75 paved mile to Township Street to its current western terminus (there's limited parking on nearby Polte Road). Trail advocates are working to someday extend the trail to Burlington. Eastward from the main trailhead, the Cascade Trail crosses Fruitdale Road and becomes crushed gravel and dirt. Mileage posts are sporadic.

The trail at first runs close to SR 20, eventually angling south and away from the busy roadway. It crosses a couple of creeks and traverses active farms. After crossing Minkler Road, the trail makes a bridged crossing of Coal Creek at 3.5 miles—a good turnaround spot. From there it contin-ues across more farms, crosses Hoehn Road, and then cuts through an area prone to flooding. Prepare for wet feet here in the winter months.

The trail then travels through its most scenic section. Cross Minkler Lake, an oxbow lake teeming with birds and pro-tected by the Skagit Land Trust. The trust has been active in protecting miles of Skagit River shoreline. You'll pass through a couple more of their properties. The trail eventually swings right to the Skagit River bank, providing stunning views of the river and surrounding Cascades foothills.

At 7.5 miles, reach Main Street in Lyman, where you can walk a couple blocks south to check out the Minkler Man-sion. The trail continues east, paralleling the Lyman Hamilton Road, traversing woodlots and crossing a couple of creeks on small trestles. At 11 miles, cross Petit Street in Hamilton. The way then crosses a slough and makes a slight detour on the road at another slough where a trestle is washed out.

At 12.2 miles, cross SR 20, exercising extreme caution as there are no crosswalks or warning lights. From here the trail passes by a bison farm and stays fairly close to SR 20 and several residences. At 16 miles, come to Baker Lake Road. Here you must carefully walk the shoulder of SR 20 to cross Grandy Creek. Then you can get back on the trail and continue east, mainly through forest.

At about 18.7 miles the trail climbs a hillside above and away from SR 20. It passes through an interesting cut in ledges and a seasonal cascade before traversing a former winery with some views. The trail then returns to the forest before reaching Concrete at 22 miles. The way continues another half mile, passing Concrete's historic, signature cement silos before ending near the town center at the old depot, now serving as a senior center.

GO FARTHER

There's a gravel and paved 1.7-mile stretch of trail alongside SR 20 just east of downtown Burlington. Its proximity to the busy highway makes it a noisy trail. But if you are in town and need to stretch your legs, it offers a traffic-free route to do so.

Next page: *Sweeping Salish Sea view from Juniper Point*

ANACORTES
AND FIDALGO
ISLAND

The city of Anacortes is situated on Fidalgo Island in western Skagit County, connected to the mainland by State Route 20's twin bridges (and by the Rainbow Bridge in La Conner). It was founded in the late 1800s with the hope—never realized—of becoming the western terminus of a transcontinental railroad. But the city soon afterward flourished as a mill and cannery town. And in the 1950s two large oil refineries were built on nearby March Point. The canneries and most of the mills are now gone, but the city's economy is flourishing thanks to boat building and recreation. Anacortes is attracting many retirees and newcomers due to its gorgeous location and growing trail, park, and outdoor recreation scene.

Anacortes is surrounded by greenbelts and water, and trails radiate from the city's downtown, hugging coastal shorelines and connecting with Fidalgo's forested hills and quiet inland bodies of water. Anacortes and Fidalgo Island contain more than 5000 acres of green spaces, including one of the largest municipal-owned forests in the region, the Anacortes Community Forest Lands (ACFL). The ACFL's more than 2800 acres of forest, wetlands, lakes, and small peaks are all within minutes of Skagit County's second largest community. Once used to protect the city's water supply, the ACFL is now a natural and recreational gem with 50-plus miles of trails. The ACFL trails can be confusing so be sure to purchase a detailed map of the ACFL, produced by the non-profit Friends of the Forest and available from retailers throughout Anacortes and online (see Appendix I).

35 **Kukutali Preserve (Kiket Island)**

DISTANCE:	2 miles of trails
ELEVATION GAIN:	Up to 180 feet
HIGH POINT:	165 feet
DIFFICULTY:	Easy
FITNESS:	Walkers and hikers
FAMILY-FRIENDLY:	Yes
DOG-FRIENDLY:	Dogs prohibited
AMENITIES:	Privy, interpretive signs
CONTACT/MAP:	Swinomish Indian Tribal Community, Washington State Parks
GPS:	N 48° 25.255" W 122° 33.209"
BEFORE YOU GO:	A Discover Pass is required; the preserve is open 6:30 am to dusk.

GETTING THERE

Driving: From exit 230 on I-5 in Burlington, head west on State Route 20 for 9.8 miles. Then turn left onto Reservation Road and drive 1.6 miles, bearing right onto Snee Oosh Road. Continue for 1.5 miles to parking and the trailhead on your right.

Located in Similk Bay and connected to Fidalgo Island by a tombolo (a spit that connects an island to the mainland), Kiket Island contains over two miles of prime shoreline and a wildlife-rich lagoon. Traditional land of the Swinomish Tribe, Kiket Island was once considered as a nuclear-power plant site before becoming a private retreat for a local vintner. In 2010 the island, along with nearby Flagstaff Island, was purchased by Washington State Parks with the help of the Trust for Public Land for $14.3 million. Given the name Kukutali (meaning cattail or cattail mat), the new 83-acre preserve is co-owned and co-managed with the Swinomish

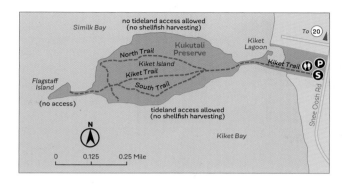

Tribe—the first tribal state park in America jointly managed by a tribe and state government agency.

GET MOVING

This special place is managed as both a wildlife and cultural preserve; please respect all posted rules and regulations. Start your exploration by walking down the Kiket Trail, once a private gravel driveway to an estate on the island. Approach the tombolo connecting Kiket to Fidalgo Island. Look south at Kiket Bay and north at Kiket Lagoon for a myriad of bird species. Reaching the forested island, the trail slowly climbs up toward the center.

At about 0.5 mile, reach a junction. Here the South Trail diverges left, meeting back up with the Kiket Trail in 0.4 mile, and the North Trail diverges right, reconnecting with the Kiket Trail in 0.5 mile. Both are worth checking out. The North Trail is more difficult climbing, close to the island's 170-foot high point. It also traverses old growth and a bald sporting showy seasonal flowers and rare plants and passes a good view of Similk Bay and Deception Pass.

All three trails bring you to a small clearing that once contained the island's former occupant's residency. Here find a privy and two more options for continuing your

Tombolo connecting Flagstaff Island to Kiket Island

explorations. You can take the Beach Trail south for 0.1 mile to the island's southern shoreline, which is open to beach walking (but no harvesting). Note, the island's northern shore is off-limits to exploring.

The Kiket Trail continues west from this spot, heading along the tombolo connecting Kiket to tiny Flagstaff Island. Flagstaff is off-limits to visitors due to its sensitive environment. But a hike along the sandy tombolo will give you a close-up view of Flagstaff, as well as a great view of the northern shore of Kiket Island and good views south into Kiket Bay of Skagit and Hope islands.

The tribe owns harvesting rights to the preserve's shoreline. They historically used the island for shellfish gathering and seining for salmon. Kukutali, or "place of cattail mat," refers to the temporary shelters constructed of cattail mats that tribal members once used while harvesting. As the tribe had long been denied access to this traditional land, the designation of the area as a preserve to be managed by both state parks and the tribe has in essence brought the island full circle for the Swinomish people. Respect it and cherish its beauty.

36 Tommy Thompson Trail

DISTANCE:	3.3 miles one-way
ELEVATION GAIN:	None
HIGH POINT:	20 feet
DIFFICULTY:	Easy
FITNESS:	Walkers and runners
FAMILY-FRIENDLY:	Yes, with paved, level trail suitable for jogging strollers and wheelchairs
DOG-FRIENDLY:	On leash
AMENITIES:	Benches, privy, interpretive signs, water
CONTACT/MAP:	City of Anacortes Parks and Recreation, Green Trails, Deception Pass Anacortes Community Forest Lands: 41S
GPS:	N 48° 30.804" W 122° 36.644"

GETTING THERE

Driving: From exit 230 on I-5 in Burlington, head west on State Route 20 for 11.7 miles to the junction with SR 20-Spur. Continue right on SR 20-Spur to Anacortes for 2.6 miles and turn right (just before the traffic circle) onto R Avenue. Continue on R Avenue, which eventually becomes Q Avenue for 1.4 miles to Cap Sante Marina and parking areas near the trail's northern terminus. Other parking areas for the trail include 34th Street and the Fidalgo Bay Resort (limited) off of Fidalgo Bay Road.

Transit: Skagit Transit (SKAT) Route 410 stops near the Northern Trailhead.

A popular paved rail trail connecting Anacortes's Old Town to March Point, nearly half of this route travels along Fidalgo Bay shoreline. The trail's southern and eastern stretch is exceptionally beautiful, utilizing a causeway and restored wooden trestle to cross the wildlife-rich bay. Nature lovers of all ages will love looking for herons, loons, grebes, otters,

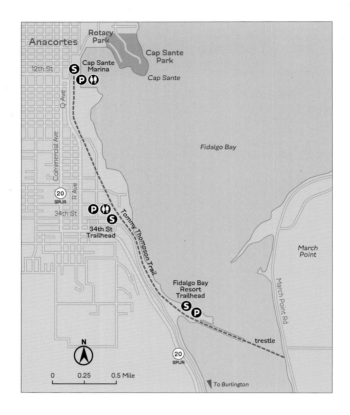

and seals along the way in the bay's sparkling waters and glistening mudflats. Enjoy good views too, of Mount Baker, Cap Sante, Guemes Island, and Hat Island. And there are interpretive signs, a totem pole, and an otter sculpture on the trail to admire.

GET MOVING

Named after a local railroad enthusiast, the Tommy Thompson Trail follows an abandoned rail line for 3.3 miles from

March Point to Old Town Anacortes. It is popular with local bicyclists, runners, and walkers. The northern reaches of the trail travel primarily through old industrial lots and shipyards; the southern section, however, travels right along the shoreline of Fidalgo Bay—and then crosses it to March Point.

From the Cap Sante Marina the trail parallels Q Avenue before passing through a skate park and then cutting across industrial lots. The trail passes near the Anacortes Marina and crosses a few roads; none of them are heavily traveled, but always exercise caution upon reaching them. At 1.2 miles, pass the Soroptimist Station Trailhead, complete with privies. At 1.4 miles reach the 34th Street Trailhead, a good starting point for doing the more interesting southern and eastern reaches of this trail.

The trail soon comes to a picnic area right on the bay. This stretch of shoreline was once heavily industrialized—and polluted. But government officials and conservationists have recently been transforming it into parkland and grounds for cleaner businesses. Take time here to read the first of several interpretive signs. And be sure to admire the beautiful otter sculpture. Then look in the calm waters for a possible real otter sighting.

Now traveling alongside the bay, pass a large private residence and cross the lawns of the Fidalgo Bay Resort, a beautiful camping area owned by the Samish Indian Nation. At 2.4 miles come to a totem pole, resort access road, and another trailhead (limited parking; privy available). Continue on the trail to its best part—out onto a causeway and trestle for nearly one mile across Fidalgo Bay.

Despite the presence of two large refineries on March Point, wildlife viewing is excellent here. Watch for otters and eagles. In low tides, look for birds on the extensive mudflats. During the winter months, loons and other wintering waterfowl can be spotted in the bay. At 2.9 miles, reach a restored wooden trestle, the highlight of the hike. Wander across it

Running on the trestle across Fidalgo Bay

for 0.4 mile, reaching the trail's end at March Point Road (no parking). Then turn around and retrace your steps.

GO FARTHER

From the trail's northern terminus at the Cap Sante Marina, walk 0.4 mile through the marina to Rotary Park. Here you can access short trails through Cap Sante Park. From Rotary Park also consider walking 0.7 mile along T Avenue, 4th Street, V Avenue, and W Avenue to the 200-foot-plus headland Cap Sante. Then take in spectacular views of Fidalgo Bay, March Point, and Mount Baker.

37 Guemes Channel and Ship Harbor Trails

DISTANCE:	2.7 miles
ELEVATION GAIN:	Minimal
HIGH POINT:	10 feet
DIFFICULTY:	Easy
FITNESS:	Walkers and runners
FAMILY-FRIENDLY:	Yes, with paved, level trail, suitable for jogging strollers and wheelchairs
DOG-FRIENDLY:	On leash
AMENITIES:	Benches, privy, interpretive signs
CONTACT/MAP:	City of Anacortes Parks and Recreation
GPS:	N 48° 30.230" W 122° 40.210"

GETTING THERE

Driving: From exit 230 on I-5 in Burlington, head west on State Route 20 for 11.7 miles to the junction with SR 20-Spur. Continue right on SR 20-Spur to Anacortes (passing through the traffic circle and following Commercial Ave), coming to a traffic light and junction with 12th Street in 4 miles. Turn left, continuing on SR 20-Spur (12th Street becoming Oakes Avenue after the D Avenue junction) for 2.7 miles. Then turn right onto Ship Harbor Boulevard (into the San Juan Passage housing development), coming to a junction in 0.1 mile. Turn left onto Edwards Way continuing to the road's end and trailhead at 0.2 mile.

Transit: Skagit Transit (SKAT) Route 410 stops at Roadside Park, where a connector trail leads to Guemes Channel Trail.

Explore two fairly new and delightfully scenic, family-friendly shoreline trails between the Washington State Ferry terminal and the Skagit County Guemes Island Ferry terminal in Anacortes. The Guemes Channel Trail is a paved path along

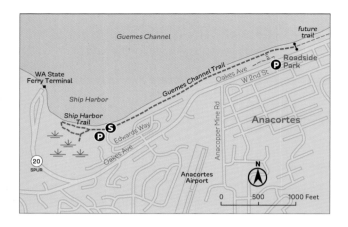

the Guemes Channel providing excellent views of Guemes, Cypress, and Lummi islands. The Ship Harbor Trail utilizes a boardwalk through a preserve of rich wetlands bordering a beautiful sandy beach. Both offer excellent opportunities for bird and marine mammal watching and for watching the Salish Sea extinguish the evening sun.

GET MOVING

From the trailhead, choose between the two trails, or take one and then the other. The paved Guemes Channel Trail heads east on a nearly level shoreline-hugging course. Enjoy exceptional views of Cypress and Guemes islands across the channel and glimpses too of Blakely and Lummi islands and Entrance Mountain on Orcas Island. Stop at interpretive signs and admire the big stately trees lining the steep slope on the south and shading the path with their overhanging branches.

At 0.8 mile, reach a junction. If you're looking for a little more cardiovascular work, consider heading right up the long stairway. Then continue on a trail left. Ignore the trail right, which leads to a subdivision. The way left soon comes to more stairs, delivering you to little Roadside Park. Now descend

Walking along the Guemes Channel Trail offers good views of Guemes Island in the background.

100 feet, returning to the Guemes Channel Trail and adding 0.2 mile to your distance total.

The Guemes Channel Trail continues east for another 0.2 mile, coming to a gate. But the good news is that the gate should be gone by late 2017 and the next phase of this trail—a 1-mile stretch to the Guemes Island Ferry—should be in place. Locals, community leaders, and trail advocates have been working hard to extend this trail east all the way to downtown Anacortes, connecting it with the Tommy Thompson Trail (Trail 36), and west all the way to Washington Park (Trail 38). For now, however, be content with the mile in place, and retrace your steps to the trailhead.

At the trailhead, the Ship Harbor Trail heads west into the Ship Harbor Interpretive Preserve. Protecting important habitat, the preserve also protects a historic site that once harbored a warship, provided the Samish people with fish, and housed some of the largest salmon canneries in the world.

Follow the wide, smooth, natural-surface path through a small wetland and along a gorgeous sandy beach. The trail meanders through thick vegetation, passing splendid viewpoints of the harbor and the nearby Washington State Ferry terminal. Several points allow access to the beach, which makes for some fine walking when tides are low. The trail continues on a boardwalk through an ecologically important wetland (stay on the trail), ending at 0.35 mile. When funding is secured, the trail will continue to the ferry terminal, giving folks waiting for a ferry to the San Juans or Sidney, BC, a nice place to get a short walk in before setting sail.

38 Washington Park

DISTANCE:	More than 4 miles
ELEVATION GAIN:	Up to 500 feet
HIGH POINT:	260 feet
DIFFICULTY:	Easy to moderate
FITNESS:	Walkers, runners and hikers
FAMILY-FRIENDLY:	Yes, but use caution on shoreline cliffs
DOG-FRIENDLY:	On leash
AMENITIES:	Benches, privy, interpretive signs, water, campground
CONTACT/MAP:	City of Anacortes Parks and Recreation
GPS:	N 48° 29.926" W 122° 41.570"

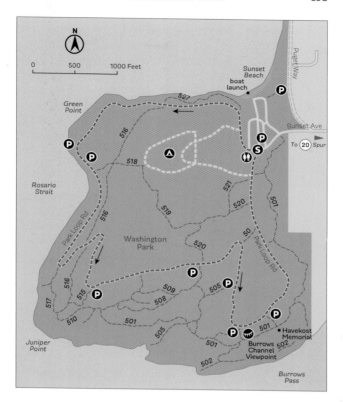

GETTING THERE

Driving: From exit 230 on I-5 in Burlington, head west on State Route 20 for 11.7 miles to the junction with SR 20-Spur. Continue right on SR 20-Spur to Anacortes (passing through the traffic circle) coming to a traffic light and junction with 12th Street in 4 miles. Turn left, continuing on SR 20-Spur for 3.1 miles to the junction with the ferry access road. Continue straight onto Sunset Avenue for 0.9 mile to day-use parking in Washington Park.

Occupying 220 acres on Fidalgo Head, the beloved and popular Washington Park offers some of the most stunning maritime scenery on the Salish Sea. You can run or walk its 2.2-mile loop road (it is closed to vehicles from dusk or 10:00 PM to 10:00 AM) and hike miles of well-maintained trails. Wander through quiet forest groves and across grassy balds that burst with spring wildflowers. And explore hidden coves harboring plenty of wildlife and sensational seaside views.

GET MOVING

Several miles of trails crisscross and encircle this gorgeous park on Fidalgo Head jutting into Rosario Strait. Although they are well maintained, they are not well marked, so be sure to download a map (which is good) and take it along with you. While most of the terrain is kid friendly, be especially careful on trails leading to ledges above the water where drops are precipitous and a fall can have serious consequences. You can loop around the park or head out and back to coves, bluffs, viewpoints, and historic sites.

Walkers and runners will definitely want to take the park's narrow, paved, tree-lined road. It's open to automobiles (one-way, 10 mph speed limit) after 10:00 AM, but don't let that discourage you. This is one of the most popular walking routes in the area, with pedestrians outnumbering all other users. It's safe to walk and absolutely gorgeous, with a lot of options for explorations—and it accesses just about every trail within the park, allowing for more loop options.

From the small day-use parking area (if full, find more parking near the playfields east of the boat launch), walk counterclockwise with the flow of traffic (recommended, though you can go either way), passing the park's popular campground to the left and pretty Sunset Beach to the right. It's fairly level to Green Point, with its gorgeous San Juan Islands views. The road then starts climbing high bluffs above the surf.

Two walkers enjoy a view of Mount Erie from the Burrows Pass Viewpoint.

At 0.8 mile, the road makes a sharp hairpin turn. Here Trail no. 517 leads to Juniper Point at the tip of Fidalgo Head. Continue up the road and soon come to Trail no. 516. You can follow this trail left through attractive forest and return to the road near Green Point, or veer onto Trail no. 518 and head to the campground. If you follow Trail no. 516 right it leads to Trail no. 510, one of the prettiest trails in the park. You can follow that trail atop open bluffs and across grassy slopes bursting with wildflowers in spring and granting breathtaking views of Rosario Strait, Lopez Island, Burrows Island, and Mount Erie. You can also take several side trails from it to more views and a remote cove. Trail no. 510 eventually turns northward, passing some of the biggest trees in the park before returning to the day-use parking area.

If you continue up the road, you'll switchback right and then left. At the second switchback, Trail no. 515 (right after an impressive memorial bench) leads right to Juniper Point (and also connects with Trail no. 510). The road continues east, passing another three trails leading left and two leading right, including Trail no. 520, which leads into the heart of the park. The road climbs to an elevation of 260 feet, then drops 80 feet, passing through a majestic grove of big cedars before climbing again. At 1.6 miles it reaches the Burrows Pass viewpoint (elev. 230 feet), one of the best overlooks in the park.

At this juniper- and madrona-graced grassy, open bluff, savor views of Mount Erie and across Burrows Pass to bulky Burrows Island. Trails here connect to Trail no. 501 and lead down the steep bluff to ledges above the channel. There are also some interpretive panels here, explaining the history of the park.

The road now descends, soon coming to a short trail south leading to the Havekost Memorial, honoring the pioneer who in 1911 donated the first parcel to what would become this beautiful park. The road continues down, passing through thick second-growth forest with big old stumps. It also passes several connecting trails to Trail no. 501 and a couple of trails leading left into the park's heart. At 2.2 miles the road completes its loop near the boat trailer parking area.

39 Sugar Loaf, Mount Erie, and Whistle Lake

DIFFICULTY:	Easy to difficult
FITNESS:	Walkers, runners, and hikers
FAMILY-FRIENDLY:	Yes, but note that trails are open to bikes and horses
DOG-FRIENDLY:	On leash
AMENITIES:	Privies, benches
CONTACT/MAP:	City of Anacortes Parks and Recreation
GPS:	N 48° 28.069" W 122° 37.776"

GETTING THERE

Driving to Sugar Loaf and Mount Erie: From exit 230 on I-5 in Burlington, head west on State Route 20 for 11.7 miles to the junction with SR 20-Spur. Go left on SR 20 and after 1.8 miles turn right onto Campbell Lake Road. Follow for 1.5 miles, bearing right onto Heart Lake Road. Continue 1.5 miles, turning right at a sign indicating "Mt. Erie Viewpoint." Proceed a couple of hundred feet (do not turn right up Mount Erie Road) to the trailhead (elev. 390 feet).

Driving to Whistle Lake: From exit 230 on I-5 in Burlington, head west on SR 20 for 11.7 miles to the junction with SR 20-Spur. Continue right on SR 20-Spur to Anacortes for 2.7 miles, turning left through the traffic circle onto Commercial Avenue heading south. After 0.4 mile, turn left onto Fidalgo Avenue and proceed for 0.2 mile. Turn left onto St. Mary's Drive, which soon becomes Hillcrest Drive, and continue for 0.3 mile. Turn right onto Whistle Lake Road and follow for 0.9 mile, turning left onto Whistle Lake Terrace. Then immediately turn right onto a dirt road and reach the trailhead (elev. 380 feet) at the road's end in 0.3 mile.

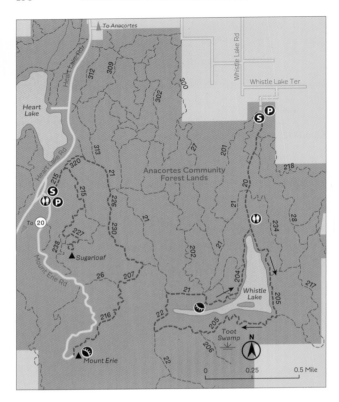

SUGARLOAF
ROUNDTRIP LOOP: 2.5 miles
ELEVATION GAIN: 650 feet
DIFFICULTY: moderate
HIGH POINT: 1044 feet

The hike or run up Sugarloaf—Fidalgo Island's second highest summit—is short and sweet, with big trees; sunny, open, south-facing slopes; and sweeping Salish Sea views.

GET MOVING
Follow Trail 215 through a swampy draw graced with a few big Douglas firs and cedars. In 0.2 mile, bear right, continuing on

Trail no. 215, and start climbing—steeply at times. At 0.5 mile, stay right at a junction and continue climbing under a canopy of mature Douglas firs, working your way up and around a series of mossy ledges.

At 1 mile, encounter yet another junction. Trail no. 215 continues straight, descending Sugarloaf's south face and reaching the Mount Erie Road in 0.3 mile. Go left through a stile and follow hiker-only Trail no. 227 for about 0.1 mile to another junction. Turn right here onto Trail no. 238, soon arriving on the blocky summit of 1044-foot Sugarloaf. Pass Trail no. 228 (which connects back with Trail no. 215) and shortly afterward come to a spur trail branching right. Follow it to sunny ledges and some sweet viewing of Whidbey, Burrows, Allan, and Lopez islands—and Mount Erie, highest point on Fidalgo Island.

MOUNT ERIE

ROUNDTRIP LOOP:	5.2 miles	**DIFFICULTY:**	difficult
ELEVATION GAIN:	910 feet	**HIGH POINT:**	1273 feet

Stand above precipitous cliffs on the highest point on Fidalgo Island and watch falcons and hang gliders ride thermals above sparkling Campbell Lake below. There's a road to Mount Erie's summit—so prepare to share the summit with many who didn't "earn it."

GET MOVING

Begin on Trail no. 215. In 0.2 mile, head left on Trail no. 320, traversing a beautiful grove of old-growth cedar. At 0.4 mile, turn right onto Trail no. 21 near a monster Douglas fir. Then follow this old fire road on a steady ascent, coming to a junction at 0.8 mile. Bear right onto Trail no. 226—then soon afterward left onto Trail no. 230 and hike through a low gap. Stay left at the next junction and enjoy easy walking, descending into a ravine above a bubbling creek, reaching a junction at 1.4 miles.

View of Campbell Lake and Skagit Bay from Mount Erie's summit

Turn right onto Trail no. 207 and switchback upward, reaching a junction at 1.6 miles. Here Trail no. 26 heads right 0.3 mile to Mount Erie Road, offering a much shorter and easier alternative approach to this hike. Continue left through a stile onto hiker-only Trail no. 216 and start winding your way up. The way is rough in sections, and you'll pass several confusing unmarked trails—stay left at all of these junctions.

Briefly brush alongside the road before making a final pitch over ledges and through thick forest. Bear left at a junction just below the summit, reaching the road at 2.5 miles. Then turn left and walk a short distance on the road to several developed viewpoints. The one east, overlooking March Point and Fidalgo Bay, is becoming grown in. Spend your time instead at the busy overlook south near the communications towers. The view is excellent southwest to Whidbey Island, east to Glacier Peak and Three Fingers, and southeast to Mount Rainier. Great views too, of Skagit Bay, with Kiket, Skagit, and Hope islands and of Campbell Lake directly below the mountain's north face. The lake's little island is the largest island on a lake on an island in Washington state.

Peregrine falcons nest in the cliffs below. Rock climbers can often be seen clambering up them. Big birds thundering from the Whidbey Island Naval Air Station can often be observed from here too.

WHISTLE LAKE

ROUNDTRIP LOOP:	4.3 miles	**DIFFICULTY:**	moderate
ELEVATION GAIN:	400 feet	**HIGH POINT:**	580 feet

The second largest lake within the ACFL, Whistle Lake once provided Anacortes with its drinking water. Today it is a popular swimming and fishing hole. Steep ledges and beautiful tracts of old-growth forest surround it. And a nice trail system allows you to circumnavigate it.

GET MOVING

Follow Trail no. 20, a wide service road beneath a thick forest canopy, passing by a few giant Douglas firs. Ignore side trails and reach a major junction complete with a privy at 0.6 mile. Continue on Trail no. 20 another 0.1 mile, coming to a junction with Trail no. 204 (Kenny Oakes Trail) at a cove on Whistle Lake.

You'll be returning on the right, so go straight, coming to the end of the old service road at a swimming area on the lake—a good destination for a short hike. To loop around the lake, pick up Trail no. 205 and follow it along the rugged shoreline, ignoring radiating side trails. Pass a few lakeside ledges granting good views of Mount Erie before crossing a creek and steeply climbing up and over a ledge. Then cross a small earthen dam. Skirt the Toot Swamp on your left, coming to a junction with Trail no. 206 at 2.2 miles. Continue on Trail no. 205, steeply climbing and coming to a junction at 2.5 miles.

Turn right onto Trail no. 22, dropping to a swampy cove before steeply climbing alongside a creek, reaching another junction shortly afterward. Turn right here onto wide Trail no. 21 and after passing Trail no. 202 on the left, reach a junction at 2.8 miles. Head right here onto Trail no. 204, losing elevation and soon coming to a large ledge overlooking the lake. After enjoying the view, continue on Trail no. 204, traveling alongside the lake passing up and over some ledges. At 3.6 miles return to Trail no. 20. Turn left and head 0.7 mile back to the trailhead.

40 Heart Lake

DISTANCE:	3 miles roundtrip
ELEVATION GAIN:	160 feet
HIGH POINT:	500 feet
DIFFICULTY:	Easy
FITNESS:	Walkers, runners, and hikers
FAMILY-FRIENDLY:	Yes, but be aware that trails are multi-use
DOG-FRIENDLY:	On leash
AMENITIES:	Privies, benches
CONTACT/MAP:	City of Anacortes Parks and Recreation
GPS:	N 48° 28.069" W 122° 37.776"

GETTING THERE
Driving: Follow directions for Trail 39, passing Mt. Erie Road and continuing north another 0.5 mile to the trailhead at the boat launch on the left (elev. 340 feet).

Grandest of the bodies of water within the ACFL, this heart-shaped lake's best feature is its enveloping old-growth forest—one of the finest stands in the Puget lowlands.

A hiker admires an ancient Douglas fir at Heart Lake.

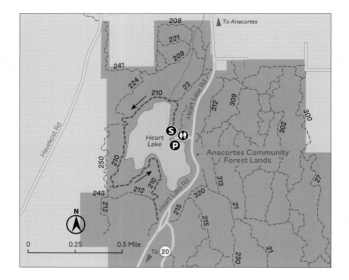

GET MOVING

Start by following Trail no. 210 north, passing several large Douglas firs along the lakeshore. At 0.2 mile, reach the first of many junctions. Bear left and shortly afterward turn left onto an old woods road, still Trail no. 210.

Cross Heart Lake's outlet creek, enjoying good views across the lake to Sugarloaf. Bear left, leaving the old road but continuing on Trail no. 210. Now stay on this trail, rounding the lake's marshy southwestern cove and coming to magnificent ancient groves of giant cedars and firs. At 1.8 miles, turn left onto Trail no. 212 and follow it 0.3 mile to Heart Lake Road. Now either walk north on the road (use caution) 0.7 mile back to the trailhead, or cross the road and proceed to the Sugarloaf trailhead. Then follow Trail no. 215 0.2 mile to Trail no. 320 and start climbing. Bear right onto Trail no. 21 and climb some more, then turn left onto Trail no. 313 and follow it downhill back to the road, crossing to the Heart Lake trailhead.

41   Little Cranberry Lake

DISTANCE:	1.9 miles roundtrip
ELEVATION GAIN:	100 feet
HIGH POINT:	325 feet
DIFFICULTY:	Easy
FITNESS:	Walkers, runners, and hikers
FAMILY-FRIENDLY:	Yes, but be aware that trails are multi-use
DOG-FRIENDLY:	On leash
AMENITIES:	Benches
CONTACT/MAP:	City of Anacortes Parks and Recreation
GPS:	N 48° 28.069" W 122° 37.776"

GETTING THERE

Driving: From exit 230 on I-5 in Burlington, head west on State Route 20 for 11.7 miles to the junction with SR 20-Spur. Continue right on SR 20-Spur to Anacortes (passing the traffic circle and following Commercial Avenue), coming to the traffic light and the junction with 12th Street in 4 miles. Turn left, continuing on SR 20-Spur (12th Street becoming Oakes Avenue after D Avenue junction) for 1.6 miles. Turn left onto Georgia Avenue. Continue for 0.2 mile, turning right onto a gravel road (signed for the ACFL). Follow for 0.3 mile to the trailhead (elev. 290 feet).

Stroll around a wildlife-rich little lake through groves of handsome firs and thick patches of salal and over sunny shoreline ledges. Surrounded by big trees and cradling two boggy islands, Little Cranberry Lake is an attractive body of water. Watch for eagles, beavers, and otters during your visit.

GET MOVING

This loop around wildlife-rich Little Cranberry Lake is almost entirely on hiker-only trails. Start by hiking east on Trail no. 100, crossing an earthen dam built in the early 1900s, which

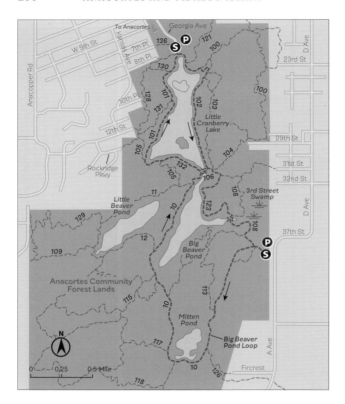

transformed this wetland depression into a shallow lake. The way hugs the lakeshore beneath mature Douglas firs and through a thick understory of ferns and salal. Stay right at a junction and come to an observation deck.

At 0.2 mile, head right onto Trail no. 102 and continue hugging the shoreline. Stay to the right at all junctions (and there are many) on this route, keeping the lakeshore always in view.

Through jumbled boulders, beneath ledges, and right along the water's edge, mosey along the lakeshore. Scan the boggy islands, one on each end of the lake, for avian

Tall timber casts a pretty reflection on Little Cranberry Lake.

and small mammal activity. You'll probably also notice some evidence of a 2016 forest fire.

At 0.8 mile, reach a junction. Head right, crossing a bridge over an inlet stream and immediately come to another junction. Go right on Trail no. 132, negotiating a short rocky section beneath a ledge, then resume easier walking. At 1.1 miles, bear right at a junction onto Trail no. 105. Cross a creek and come to another junction, taking Trail no. 101 right along the lake's west shoreline. Climb up and over some sunny ledges before completing the loop at 1.9 miles.

42   Big Beaver Pond and Mitten Pond

DISTANCE:	2.7 miles roundtrip
ELEVATION GAIN:	120 feet
HIGH POINT:	370 feet
DIFFICULTY:	Easy
FITNESS:	Walkers, runners, and hikers
FAMILY-FRIENDLY:	Yes, but be aware that trails are multi-use
DOG-FRIENDLY:	On leash
AMENITIES:	Viewing platform
CONTACT/MAP:	City of Anacortes Parks and Recreation
GPS:	N 48° 28.069" W 122° 37.776"

GETTING THERE

Driving: From exit 230 on I-5 in Burlington, head west on SR 20 for 11.7 miles to the junction with SR 20-Spur. Continue right on SR 20-Spur for 2.7 miles to Anacortes; at the traffic circle, head right onto Commercial Avenue (SR 20-Spur). In 0.2 mile, turn left at the traffic light onto 32nd Street. Continue 0.8 mile to D Avenue and turn left. Follow this arterial (which curves right in 0.3 mile to become 37th and then turns left in 0.2 mile to become A Avenue) 0.5 mile to the trailhead (elev. 300 feet).

Boardwalk at Big Beaver Pond

Wander aimlessly and easily on a network of trails around two small ponds and through a network of wetlands. Come in spring for woodland blossoms or in the fall for yellow-brushed shrubbery streaking the enveloping dark green forest. Look for beavers, coyotes, ducks, and eagles in this wildlife haven.

GET MOVING

Start your trip around this wildlife-rich wetland on Trail 10, an old woods road. In 0.1 mile pass Trail 108, which you'll be returning on. Stay on Trail 10, gently climbing through a mature forest of Douglas fir, grand fir, and western red cedar.

At 0.4 mile, come to a junction with Trail no. 113, which heads right 0.4 mile to Big Beaver Pond. Continue straight, soon coming upon Mitten Pond. Pass several more trail junctions, then at 1.4 miles come to Trail no. 12, which leads to Little Beaver Pond (a good side trip). The loop continues right on Trail no. 10. Soon see Big Beaver Pond on your right (more of a swamp), and at 1.7 miles yet another junction. The old road swings sharply left now as Trail no. 11, leading to Little Beaver Pond. Take the single track Trail no. 106 right, reaching an arm of Big Beaver at the water's level. At 1.8 miles, come to a junction at Little Cranberry Lake. Head right on Trail no. 104, crossing the creek connecting Cranberry to Big Beaver. Then climb a small rise, ignoring Trail no. 102 to the left. At 1.9 miles, come to a junction with Trails no. 103 and 108. Head right on Trail no. 108 and soon come to Trail no. 123 on the right.

Pass through the stile and enjoy this hiker-only path along the shores of Big Beaver Pond. Reach Trail no. 108 and take it to the right, crossing a bridge. Skirt the 32nd Street Swamp and continue through big firs and cedars, passing two side trails and returning to Trail no. 10 at 2.6 miles. The trailhead is 0.1 mile to the left.

43 Deception Pass State Park

FITNESS:	Walkers, runners, and hikers
FAMILY-FRIENDLY:	Yes, but use caution on shoreline cliffs
DOG-FRIENDLY:	On leash
AMENITIES:	Benches, privy, interpretive signs, water, campground
CONTACT/MAP:	Deception Pass State Park
	Green Trails, Deception Pass Anacortes
	Community Forest Lands: 41S
GPS:	N 48° 24.997" W 122° 39.072"
BEFORE YOU GO:	A Discover Pass is required.

GETTING THERE

Driving to Pass Lake: From exit 230 on I-5 in Burlington, head west on State Route 20 for 11.7 miles to the junction with SR 20-Spur. Continue left on SR 20 for 5.1 miles, turning right onto Rosario Road. Then immediately turn right into the Pass Lake boat launch and trailhead (elev. 130 feet).

Driving to Rosario Head, Lighthouse, and Lottie Points: From exit 230 on I-5 in Burlington, head west on SR 20 for 11.7 miles to the junction with SR 20-Spur. Continue left on

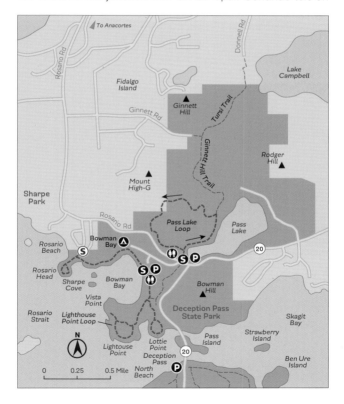

SR 20 for 5.1 miles, turning right onto Rosario Road. Proceed 100 yards and then immediately turn left onto Bowman Bay Road. After 0.3 mile, turn left and reach a large parking area, boat launch, and trailhead (elev. 10 feet) in 0.1 mile.

Washington's most visited state park occupies more than 4100 acres on Fidalgo and Whidbey islands at Deception Pass and offers more than 40 miles of trails. Hikers, walkers, and runners will find much to their liking here. Roam on rugged coastal headlands. Explore hidden coves and tidal pools teeming with crusty critters. Wander through towering ancient evergreens and along placid lakeshore. And savor breathtaking views and nature at its finest.

GET MOVING

Note: My *Day Hiking the San Juans and Gulf Islands* contains detailed descriptions of many of the trails within Deception Pass State Park and the nearby Sharpe Park. My upcoming *Urban Trails Everett* spotlights the trails in Deception Pass State Park on Whidbey Island. Here I offer a good roundup of some of the best trails on the Fidalgo Island portion of Deception Pass State Park.

PASS LAKE
ROUNDTRIP LOOP: 2.8 miles   **DIFFICULTY:** moderate
ELEVATION GAIN: 470 feet   **HIGH POINT:** 480 feet

Except for the constant buzz of highway noise and the occasional roar of Whidbey Naval Air Station jets overhead, Pass Lake is actually a peaceful place. This is one of the quietest parts of the park in terms of foot traffic on the trails.

Follow the Pass Lake Loop (part of the Pacific Northwest Trail, or PNT) north, ascending a bench above the lake. Despite the trail's proximity to the shoreline, big trees obscure lake viewing to just glimpses. At 0.1 mile, bear right at a

A hiker traversing a grassy bluff on Lighthouse Point

junction. You'll be returning left. Lined with ferns and salal, the trail traverses a mature forest of Douglas fir, grand fir, and a few Sitka spruces.

At 0.7 mile come to a junction. The Ginnett Hill Trail (PNT) continues straight to the 1.1-mile Tursi Trail opened in 2016. Developed by the Washington Trails Association and Skagit Land Trust, this trail honors John Tursi. Born to Italian immigrants in New York in 1917, Tursi left a hardscrabble life for the Northwest to work with the Civilian Conservation Corps (CCC) at Deception Pass State Park. He later became quite a philanthropist and conservationist. He passed away in 2016 at the age of 98. His legacy lives on with this interesting trail, part of a corridor connecting Deception Pass State Park to the ACFL. Consider a side trip on it taking you over scenic open promontories and past historic sites.

The Pass Lake Loop heads left on an old fire road winding through thick forest. Climb to about 480 feet before slowly descending. Then briefly leave the park, passing through a recent timber harvest. Now follow a skid road, leaving it left onto a trail at 2.4 miles. Pass through handsome old-growth forest, coming to a familiar junction in 0.3 mile. Turn right to return to your start.

ROSARIO HEAD

ROUNDTRIP:	1.7 miles	DIFFICULTY:	easy
ELEVATION GAIN:	210 feet	HIGH POINT:	90 feet

A spectacular rocky headland, Rosario Head is rife with natural beauty and human history.

From the boat launch parking area, head right (west) across grassy lawns, coming to the CCC Interpretive Center, open throughout the summer. Stop in to learn about what this Great Depression Era federal program, often referred to as (President Franklin D.) "Roosevelt's Tree Army," did for America.

Enjoy their legacy by hiking the trail to the west. After skirting a campground, climb high above Bowman Bay on a trail blasted into the ledge. Enjoy excellent views of the Gull Rocks below and Lighthouse Point across the bay. Then descend to a trail junction at a picnic area at 0.7 mile. Right leads to Rosario Beach and a trailhead (alternative start). Head left.

Pass a dock on Sharpe Cove and come to the Maiden of Deception Pass. In 1983, the Samish Tribe placed this 23-foot-tall carved cedar story pole here at one of their traditional tribal campsites. You can read her story, told around its base. Then follow the 0.3-mile loop up and around 60-foot-high Rosario Head. Keep children and dogs close as you walk along cliffs dropping straight to Rosario Strait. Savor spectacular views of Sares Head, Whidbey Island, the San Juan Islands, and the Olympic Mountains. Then return the way you came.

LIGHTHOUSE AND LOTTIE POINTS

ROUNDTRIP:	2.6 miles	DIFFICULTY:	easy
ELEVATION GAIN:	400 feet	HIGH POINT:	100 feet

These short trails allow you to admire Deception Pass, with its treacherous waters and historic bridge connecting Fidalgo and Whidbey islands, from a lower vantage point without the car and foot traffic on the bridge itself. Start by walking south along Bowman Bay, passing the boat launch and pier. Climb over a bluff offering good views of the bay, reaching a junction at 0.3 mile. The way left heads 0.5 mile to Pass Lake; you want to continue right, soon reaching another junction. Left goes to Lottie Point; right goes to Lighthouse Point.

Lighthouse Point: Drop back to sea level and walk along a wide tombolo. Then clamber up some ledges, entering old-growth Douglas fir forest and reaching a junction in 0.1 mile. You'll be returning right, so continue left, passing ledges and

Deception Pass Bridge from Lottie Point

grassy bluffs granting excellent views of Deception Pass and
North Beach on Whidbey Island.

The way rounds the cliffy headland just east of Lighthouse
Point, reaching an excellent viewpoint of Rosario Strait and
Lopez Island. In 0.5 mile, a side trail leads 0.2 mile left to Vista

Point, overlooking Bowman Bay. The main trail continues west through gorgeous old growth, reaching a familiar junction in 0.2 mile. Turn left, retracing your steps over the tombolo, reaching the Lottie Point Loop to Lottie Point in 0.1 mile.

Lottie Point: Follow the Lottie Point Loop through big firs along Lottie Bay, reaching a junction in 0.2 mile. The trail loops here. Continue right, steeply switchbacking up and over the 100-foot point, reaching a spur in 0.2 mile. Take the 0.1-mile return spur to a bluff at water's edge, with exceptional views of the 1935-built Deception Pass Bridge and the treacherous waters of Canoe and Deception passes. Then continue the loop, climbing once again before dropping back to a familiar junction in 0.2 mile. Turn right and return to your start in 0.3 mile.

GO FARTHER

Located on Rosario Road 1.5 miles farther northwest of Deception Pass State Park is the Sharpe Park and Montgomery-Duban Headlands County Park. Here you can hike on several miles of trails on a ruggedly beautiful stretch of undeveloped Fidalgo Island coastline. This 112-acre Skagit County Park comprises two parcels: Sharpe Park and the Montgomery-Duban Headlands. The 0.6-mile trail to Sares Head is kid and dog friendly, while the other 1.6 miles of trail in the park involve ledges and some steep descents and ascents. Use caution on these trails, especially along the spectacular coastal cliffs and ledges. The views, however, are breathtaking; they include Whidbey, Burrows, Allen, and Lopez islands and the Olympic Peninsula. The view from Sares Head includes Northwest Island, Deception Island, Rosario Head, and Lighthouse Point in Deception Pass State Park.

APPENDIX I
CONTACTS AND MAPS

Airport Trails
www.beactiveskagit.org

Anacortes Community Forest Lands
www.cityofanacortes.org/acfl_trail_maps2.php

Arroyo Park
www.cob.org/services/recreation/parks-trails
/Pages/arroyo-park.aspx

Bay to Baker Trail
www.cob.org/documents/parks/parks-trails
/trail-guide/bay_baker_trail.pdf

Berthusen Park
(360)354-6717
www.lyndenwa.org/departments/parks/#bertpark

Serene Kiket Island shoreline

Cascade Trail
www.skagitcounty.net/Departments/ParksAnd
Recreation/parks/cascadetrail.htm

Chuckanut Mountain Park
(Pine and Cedar lakes, Raptor Ridge, Chuckanut Ridge)
www.co.whatcom.wa.us/2051/Chuckanut-Mountain-Park

City of Anacortes Parks and Recreation
(360)293-1918
www.cityofanacortes.org/parks.php

City of Bellingham Parks
(360)778-7000
www.cob.org/gov/dept/parks

City of Mount Vernon Parks and Recreation
(360)336-6215
www.mountvernonwa.gov/Index.aspx

Connelly Creek Trail
www.cob.org/documents/parks/parks-trails
/trail-guide/connelly_creek.pdf

Guemes Channel and Ship Harbor trails
www.guemeschanneltrail.com

Hovander Homestead and Tennant Lake parks
www.co.whatcom.wa.us/1957
/Hovander-Homestead-Park

Interurban Trail
www.cob.org/documents/parks/parks-trails/trail-guide
/interurban.pdf

Klipsun Trail and Northridge Park
www.cob.org/documents/parks/parks-trails/trail-guide
/northridge-park.pdf

Lake Padden Park
www.cob.org/services/recreation/parks-trails/Pages
/lake-padden-park.aspx

Lake Whatcom Park
www.co.whatcom.wa.us/2098/Lake-Whatcom-Park

Larrabee State Park
(360)902-8844
parks.state.wa.us/536/Larrabee

Little Mountain Park
www.mountvernonwa.gov/Facilities/Facility/Details
/Little-Mountain-Park-15

Lookout Mountain Forest Preserve
www.co.whatcom.wa.us/2186
/Lookout-Mountain-Forest-Preserve

Mount Vernon Riverwalk
www.mountvernonwa.gov/Facilities/Facility/Details
/Skagit-Riverwalk-Park-28

Northern State Recreation Area
www.skagitcounty.net/Departments/ParksAnd
Recreation/parks/nsra.htm

Padilla Bay National Estuarine Research Reserve
(360)428-1558
www.padillabay.gov

Padilla Bay Shore Trail
www.skagitcounty.net/Departments/ParksAnd
Recreation/parks/padilla.htm

Point Whitehorn Marine Reserve
www.co.whatcom.wa.us/2108/Point-Whitehorn-Marine-Park

Port of Skagit
(360)757-0011
www.portofskagit.com

Railroad Trail
www.cob.org/documents/parks/parks-trails/trail-guide
/railroad.pdf

Semiahmoo Spit
www.co.whatcom.wa.us/2064/Semiahmoo-Park

Skagit County Parks and Recreation
(360)416-1350
www.skagitcounty.net/Departments/ParksAnd
Recreation/main.htm

South Bay Trail
www.cob.org/documents/parks/parks-trails
/trail-guide/south_bay.pdf

Squires Lake Park
www.co.whatcom.wa.us/2155/Squires-Lake-Park

Stimpson Family Nature Reserve
www.co.whatcom.wa.us/2180
/Stimpson-Family-Nature-Reserve

Swinomish Indian Tribal Community
Kukutali Preserve
(360)466-3163
www.swinomish.org/resources/environmental
-protection/kukutali-preserve.aspx

Washington Department of Fish and Wildlife (WDFW)
North Puget Sound Region 4
(425)775-1311
wdfw.wa.gov/

Washington State Department of Natural Resources
Blanchard State Forest
Northwest Region Office
(360)856-3500
www.dnr.wa.gov/Blanchard

Washington Park
www.cityofanacortes.org/washington_park.php

Washington State Parks
Deception Pass State Park
(360)675-2417
parks.state.wa.us/497/Deception-Pass

Western Washington University
Sehome Hill Arboretum
(360) 778-7000
www.wwu.edu/share

Whatcom County Parks and Recreation
(360)778-5000
www.co.whatcom.wa.us/1787/Parks-Recreation

Whatcom Falls Park
www.cob.org/services/recreation/parks-trails/Pages
/whatcom-falls-park.aspx

Overhanging sandstone cliffs on the Rock Trail

APPENDIX II
TRAIL AND CONSERVATION ORGANIZATIONS

Anacortes Parks Foundation
http://anacortesparksfoundation.org

Conservation Northwest
www.conservationnw.org

Forterra
http://forterra.org

Friends of the Forest (Anacortes Community Forest Lands)
www.friendsoftheacfl.org

Mount Vernon Trailbuilders
www.littlemountainpark.org

The Mountaineers
www.mountaineers.org

Nature Conservancy
www.nature.org

Pacific Northwest Trail
www.pnt.org

Skagit Land Trust
www.skagitlandtrust.org

SWITMO (Skagit-Whatcom-Island Trail Maintaining Organization)
www.switmo.org/index.shtml

Washington State Parks Foundation
http://wspf.org

Washington Trails Association
www.wta.org

Washington Wildlife and Recreation Coalition
www.wildliferecreation.org

Whatcom Land Trust
www.whatcomlandtrust.org

Whatcom Parks and Recreation Foundation
http://wprfoundation.org

APPENDIX III
RUNNING CLUBS AND ORGANIZED RUNS, HIKES, AND WALKS IN AND AROUND BELLINGHAM

Anacortes Art Dash
Annual 5K, 10K and half marathon utilizing the shoreline Tommy Thompson Trail.
http://anacortesartsfestival.com/special-events/art-dash-run

Bellingham Bay Marathon
Mostly flat course along Bellingham Bay including the South Bay Trail
www.bellinghambaymarathon.org/

Chuckanut 50K
Challenging and prestigious event on trails with more than 5000 vertical feet of climbing in the Chuckanut Mountains; 2017 event is the race's 25th annual.
http://chuckanut50krace.com

Greater Bellingham Running Club (GBRC)
Active running group that welcomes walkers and hosts
a dozen annual events each year—family friendly and
economical.
www.gbrc.net/

Lost Lake Ultra Run
25K and 50K runs in the Chuckanut Mountains
http://lostlakeultras.com

The Mountaineers
Seattle-based outdoors club has a Bellingham branch
involved with local conservation issues as well as
coordinating group outdoor activities.
www.mountaineers.org

Mount Baker Club
Family-friendly outdoors club that has been around
since 1911.
www.mountbakerclub.org

Skagit Runners
Active running club that sponsors more than a half-dozen
family-friendly running events annually, including the Tulip
Run, which utilizes the Skagit Airport Trails and the Lost Lake
Ultras, held on trails in the Chuckanut Mountains.
www.skagitrunners.org

Woolley Runs
Annual half marathon, marathon, and 50K race on the
Cascade Trail. Low-key, fun event followed by a BBQ.
http://skagitultrarunners.com/woolley-runs

Bald eagle nest at Skagit Wildlife Area

ACKNOWLEDGMENTS

RESEARCHING AND WRITING *URBAN TRAILS: BELLINGHAM* was fun, gratifying, and a lot of hard work. I couldn't have finished this project without the help and support of the following people. A huge thank-you to all the great people at Mountaineers Books, especially publisher Helen Cherullo, editor-in-chief Kate Rogers, managing editors Margaret Sullivan and Janet Kimball, and project manager Mary Metz.

A big thank-you to my copyeditor, Kristi Hein, for her attention to detail and thoughtful suggestions, helping to make this book a finer volume. I also want to thank my family: my wife, Heather, son, Giovanni, and parents, Richard and Judy, for accompanying me on several of the trails in this book. A big thanks, too, to Jennifer Coleman and Suzanne Gerber for providing excellent trail company. And I thank God for watching over me and keeping me safe and healthy while I hiked and ran all over Western Whatcom County and the Skagit Valley.

Spectacular view of Mount Baker from Chuckanut Ridge

INDEX

Giovanni, Craig, and Heather at Point Whitehorse

ABOUT THE AUTHOR

Craig Romano grew up in rural New Hampshire, where he fell in love with the natural world. He moved to Washington in 1989 and has since hiked more than 19,000 miles in the Evergreen State. An avid runner as well, Craig has run more than twenty-five marathons and ultra runs, including the Boston Marathon and the White River 50 Mile Endurance Run.

Craig is an award-winning author and coauthor of seventeen books; his *Columbia Highlands, Exploring Washington's Last Frontier* was recognized in 2010 by Washington Secretary of State Sam Reed and State Librarian Jan Walsh as a "Washington Reads" book for its contribution to Washington's cultural heritage. Craig also writes for numerous publications, tourism websites, and Hikeoftheweek.com.

When not hiking, running, and writing, he can be found napping with his wife, Heather; son, Giovanni; and cat, Giuseppe, at his home in Skagit County. Visit him at http://CraigRomano.com and on Facebook at Craig Romano Guidebook Author.